A Gift to: _____

From: _____

carry me over the threshold

a christian guide
to wedding traditions

kristina seleshanko

ZONDERVAN™

GRAND RAPIDS, MICHIGAN 49530 USA

ZONDERVAN.COM/
AUTHOR**TRACKER**

ZONDERVAN™

Carry Me Over the Threshold
Copyright © 2005 by Kristina Seleshanko
Illustrations Copyright © 2005 by Lyn Boyer

Requests for information should be addressed to:

Zondervan, *Grand Rapids, Michigan 49530*

Library of Congress Cataloging-in-Publication Data

Seleshanko, Kristina, 1971–
    Carry me over the threshold : a Christian guide to wedding traditions /
Kristina Seleshanko.
        p. cm.
    Includes bibliographical references and index.
    ISBN-10: 0-310-26476-6
    ISBN-13: 978-0-310-26476-7
    1. Marriage—Religious aspects—Christianity. 2. Weddings. I. Title.
BV835.S435 2005
392.5'088'27—dc22

2005008720

This edition printed on acid-free paper.

Interior design by Michelle Espinoza

Printed in the United States of America

05 06 07 08 09 10 11 • 14 13 12 11 10 9 8 7 6 5 4 3 2 1

carry me over the threshold

contents

Part One
Pre-Ceremony Traditions

Part Two
Ceremony Traditions

Part Three
Post-Ceremony Traditions

acknowledgments

no book is written without the help of many people." It's a phrase so common on acknowledgment pages, it's become trite. Nonetheless, it is 100 percent true. For example, without the initial interest of Paul Engle, this book never would have been published. And without his gentle guidance, this book wouldn't have been the same. A myriad of other people at Zondervan also helped create this book; you know who you are, and I thank each and every one of you for your contributions.

Then there are friends and colleagues who, without batting an eyelash, uncovered material that helped me weed through some of the more difficult histories; many thanks to Toby Lee Spiegel, Emily Moore, Michael Simmons, "Leli," "Juggler," and "Grimace." Thanks also to those complete strangers who took the time to read over the first draft of my manuscript and offer their reactions. For allowing this book to take up several hours of their lives, I thank Meghan Griffen, Naomi Wallace, Erin Vest, and Elizabeth Sandlin Knight. Thanks also to my mother, Gretchen Harris, and my sister, Lisa Crivello, who gave their time and energy to proofread my initial proposal and look over some of the drafts of this book. My brother, Don Adams, also read and gave encouraging words — just when I needed them; thank you. Thanks also to Rabbi Lawrence Rigal, who willingly gave his time and expertise, especially on the topic of *yichud*.

And last but not least, this book never would have even been an inkling in my mind if it weren't for my dear husband,

Alexei. It was our marriage that prompted my interest in this particular (and peculiar?) area of history and inspired me to dream of writing books about weddings. My knight in shining armor also offered endless encouragement throughout the three years it took to make this book happen. He always believed in me and prayed for me. I'm blessed to have him in my life, and I thank the Lord for him every day.

let your light shine!

"You are the light of the world. A city on a hill cannot be hidden.
Neither do people light a lamp and put it under a bowl. Instead they
put it on its stand, and it gives light to everyone in the house. In the
same way, let your light shine before men, that they may see
your good deeds and praise your Father in heaven."

Matthew 5:14–16

◆
If you're reading this book, you're probably at an exciting stage in your life; you're an engaged woman! Or perhaps you picked up this book because you're the friend or relative of a soon-to-be bride, and you're eager to help make her wedding all that much more meaningful. Or maybe you're celebrating a wedding anniversary and are curious to know a bit more about wedding customs. Whatever the case, I hope you'll find this book intriguing and helpful.

Like many brides-to-be, one of the first things I did as an engaged woman was hit the bookstores and buy every bridal magazine and book I could get my hands on. Unfortunately, I found nothing to answer my questions about the origins of wedding traditions. Oh sure, some books and magazines offered bits of information about the history of rice throwing or garter tossing, but nothing really addressed my interest in — and concerns about — wedding customs and the Christian bride. That's why I wrote this book.

So if you want to know where the tradition of wedding bells comes from, or whether unity candles really did originate on a soap opera, or whether there's any Christian meaning behind wedding rings, this book is for you.

A few people have asked me, "Why a special book for Christian brides? How are Christian couples any different from other couples?"

While most brides care about meaningful wedding traditions, Christian brides especially benefit from understanding the background behind such customs. In the New Testament, Christ tells us that we are the light of the world and that we should let that light shine before all humankind (Matt. 5:14 – 16). Christians shouldn't hide their faith; they should, according to Jesus, make sure their faith is shining brightly in front of the world.

With this in mind, some Christian couples may find that certain wedding customs don't let their light shine; these traditions may seem steeped in worldly principles they don't want to share with their friends and family on their wedding day. On the other hand, couples may discover that other customs have deep Christian meaning; these may make their wedding day even more special — and may help draw their guests closer to the Lord. (A great way to share the meaning behind traditions is to print a wedding program that lists some of the customs you're using and describes their origins.)

How This Book May Help You

As you read through *Carry Me Over the Threshold*, make note of what customs stand out to you. What touches your heart?

What holds meaning for you and your groom? These are the traditions you should consider adding to your wedding.

For example, when I was planning my own wedding, I initially thought I wouldn't bother with an aisle runner. Our wedding ceremony took place outdoors, and an aisle runner seemed unnecessarily complicated. How would I keep it from blowing away? When would it get rolled out? When would it be rolled back up? Too much trouble, it seemed to me. But then I discovered that white aisle runners have strong Christian symbolism. (You can read about this on page 66.) Suddenly, I understood why white aisle runners have a long and cherished history in Christian weddings. Suddenly, that simple white cloth took on great meaning — and I couldn't wait to use one in our wedding.

Another newlywed I know initially wanted to include traditional rice throwing at her wedding. *After all,* she thought, *everyone else does it. Isn't it expected? And it's kind of fun.* Then she discovered the roots behind the tradition (see page 86), which made her feel uncomfortable. Ultimately, she decided an alternative tradition was a better choice for her and her groom.

It's my hope you'll be similarly guided by this book. I encourage you to discover traditions that have special meaning for you and your fiancé. In the process, you may discover other traditions that just aren't what you're interested in for your big day.

And that brings up an important question: *Should Christians participate in traditions stemming from pagan rituals or other non-Christian sources?*

I believe this is a very individual decision and should be thoroughly discussed by a couple and their pastor. It's not the role of this book to stipulate which traditions should and should not be part of a Christian wedding. Instead, I hope you'll use this book to educate yourself about the history behind wedding traditions; then, through careful thought and prayer, you can decide which traditions best reflect Christian marriage and hold the most meaning for you. These traditions — and only these — should have the honor of being part of your wedding.

And while it's always an excellent idea to be educated about the original meaning behind customs, it also pays to ask yourself a couple of questions. For instance, *are all things stemming from pagan rituals forbidden to Christians?* Christians have been giving pagan practices "makeovers" for centuries. There are numerous examples of this, but I'll offer just a few.

Many of our most cherished Christmas customs (such as putting up Christmas trees and passing out gifts) have pagan origins but are now so infused with Christian meaning that some atheists and modern secularists object to them. What we now call Easter was also originally a pagan holiday, but Christians imbued it with their own religious meaning until it was no longer thought of as a pagan celebration at all. Worshiping on Sunday was also a pagan custom, but when Christ rose on a Sunday, early Christians adopted that day to praise and honor the Lord; today most Americans recognize Sunday as "church day," even if they aren't Christians.

And so it is with wedding traditions. Many stem from ancient pagan practices (although you may be surprised how many are traceable to the Bible), but that's no reason Christians can't adopt them and instill them with Christian meaning. Consider the apostle Paul's words: "One man considers one day more sacred than another; another man considers every day alike. Each one should be fully convinced in his own mind. He who regards one day as special, does so to the Lord. He who eats meat, eats to the Lord, for he gives thanks to God; and he who abstains, does so to the Lord and gives thanks to God" (Rom. 14:5–6).

As one Christian bride recently told me, "The Bible calls us to take dominion over creation; so as Christians, when we see something that doesn't glorify God, it's our job to change that thing so it can glorify Christ." It's certainly a thought worth pondering.

Is something that's traditional automatically "good"? We tend to accept traditions without much thought, but we can benefit from contemplating them. You may find that some traditions, when you stop to think about them, leave a bad taste in your mouth. You may also find that reflecting on traditions freshens their meaning for you in new and positive ways.

Few things in modern life are more tradition-filled than weddings, but just because a certain tradition is expected doesn't mean you need to include it in your wedding. Never be afraid to start new traditions if they hold more meaning for you and your groom.

*

So sit back and begin a journey that I hope you'll find as fascinating as I do. Some information contained in this book may surprise you; some may even shock you. But in any case, I hope it will enrich you — and your wedding.

part 1

pre-ceremony traditions

chapter 1

announcements and banns

Long ago, engagements and betrothals were much more public than they are today. In biblical times, Hebrews declared their matrimonial intentions to the entire community. Neighbors, friends, and family witnessed the couple's promise to marry and watched as the groom offered gifts to the bride. Often the groom's friends also gave presents — sometimes in the form of money, which helped pay for the wedding. A grand feast followed, including eating, drinking, music, and dancing.

During the Middle Ages, parents of the bride hired "barkers" — men who shouted out the wedding news for all the town to hear. Newspaper announcements of engagements and weddings started to appear in the eighteenth century. These were brief news accounts naming the couple and their parents, and sometimes stating the time and place of the wedding. Photographs didn't accompany such announcements until the early twentieth century; at that time, a photo of the bride — all by herself — was sometimes seen. Showing the couple together is a modern tradition.

Throughout most of the nineteenth century, newspaper announcements were rare; most Victorians were horrified to have their picture in the newspaper — although some engagements found their way into gossip columns. Formal handwritten notes from the bride's mother were considered the best way to announce the engagement to family and friends.

Since ancient times, "banns" have also involved the public in couples' engagements. *Banns* (an old English word meaning "to summon") are announcements of wedding intentions read from the church pulpit. They are still used in many parts of the world. Banns are said to have originated with Charlemagne — the first king to create what was called a "Christian nation." In the first several years of Charlemagne's reign (around AD 800), the number of children of dubious lineage was vast; Charlemagne was concerned that people were marrying half brothers or sisters without realizing it. Not only did this pose moral difficulties from the Christian standpoint, but it resulted in birth defects. Therefore, the king ordered that all marriages must be announced publicly so that anyone with information about the couple's lineage could come forward and stop the marriage, if necessary. Banns also helped prevent bigamy and lapses in betrothal agreements.

Banns continued as a tradition in most Christian nations — though today such readings are usually just a way to spread the good news. Although banns are virtually unknown in the United States (they largely passed out of fashion in the 1930s and '40s), they are still usually required if a couple wishes to be married in the Church of England. In Canada, couples must either obtain a state license or have banns read in church.

chapter 2

bachelor parties

traditionally, bachelor parties are thrown by the groom's friends to good-naturedly poke fun at his "last night of freedom." Some experts believe bachelor parties began in the fifteenth century, when Spartan military men would feast and toast each other the night before they married — the same way they'd feast after a soldier's death in battle. Nonetheless, while there hasn't always been a name for it, some form of the bachelor party has probably existed for most of history.

Even though drinking and philandering are closely connected to the bachelor party tradition, a more meaningful element has always graced them: the bachelor party is a way for the groom to pledge his continued friendship to his male friends, despite his change in status.

No modern groom should feel he must offend or be unfaithful to his bride at his bachelor party. In fact, today's grooms often opt for bachelor parties centered around sports or events (such as taking in a baseball game or going fishing), Bible retreats (getaways to somewhat remote areas to focus on Christian fellowship and Bible study), barbeques, or some adventure the groom has always wanted to try (such as skydiving). Whatever is chosen for the party, it should be something the groom is comfortable with, and it shouldn't keep him up late the night before the wedding. (Trust me, weddings are exhausting all by themselves!)

Bachelorette parties began popping up in the 1960s and '70s; some women felt bridal showers were dowdy and boring and wanted the alleged fun of drinking and strippers instead. Today bachelorette parties are less in fashion, and more creative bridal showers tend to be favored.

A new twist on the bachelor party is the coed get-together. Designed as a way to celebrate with friends and family of both sexes, the coed party often includes the bride as well as the groom.

chapter 3

betrothal

◆

I n biblical times, betrothals were a vital part of marriage custom. Although betrothal is sometimes defined as "engagement," a betrothal is actually a different and much more serious affair. An engaged person can break off the engagement at any time without much consequence. A betrothed person cannot legally break off the betrothal, except in rare instances.

Betrothals were binding agreements — just as binding as the marriage itself. They were agreed to among witnesses, and a contract was signed. The groom sealed the contract by giving the bride gifts; in many ancient cultures, this included a betrothal ring, a forerunner of the modern engagement ring. Sometimes, in lieu of a ring, a coin was split in two; one half was given to the groom, and one half to the bride. The betrothal ceremony was followed by a party to celebrate the upcoming marriage.

Among the ancient Hebrews, betrothals could be broken only for the biblical reasons given for divorce. For example, consider Mary and Joseph, Jesus' earthly parents. Because they were betrothed but not yet married, they didn't have the right to be sexually intimate; therefore, when Mary told Joseph she was pregnant, Joseph assumed she'd been with another man. A betrothed woman who was intimate with another man committed adultery, which is why Joseph considered "divorcing" Mary (see Matt. 1:18–19). Similarly, if a betrothed man promised to marry a second woman, he was considered a bigamist.

The Hebrew word for betrothal (*kiddushin* or *qiddushin*) means "to be set apart, or sanctified." Ancient accounts of betrothals indicate they were considered real and binding — but incomplete — marriages. In fact, betrothed couples often called themselves "husband" and "wife." Betrothal was the first step toward being married, with the wedding ceremony and con-summation being the final steps. In most cases, at least twelve months elapsed between the betrothal and the wedding.

Many scholars believe ancient Hebrews used the betrothal as the beginning of courtship. If a young man noticed a young woman who pleased him, he'd either go to his father (so the marriage could be arranged by the parents) or go directly to the girl's father (to see if he was willing to have his daughter married). If the fathers approved, the young man approached his chosen bride with a cup of wine — and in some cases, a marriage contract. The young woman read the contract (which included everything from monetary issues to promises the man made to her on a personal level), and if she liked him, she drank from the wine glass, indicating a betrothal could be formed. If she pushed the glass away, she refused his offer.

Until that time, most brides and grooms didn't know each other; therefore, the year between betrothal and marriage was a chance for the young man to woo his soon-to-be wife.

Today there is a growing trend in the Christian community to bring back betrothals; because they're a serious commitment, they protect both parties from engagements made too lightly. In some areas of the western world, a non-binding betrothal is made between couples as a public way to make a pledge of marriage; this is not the strict, legally binding action it was during biblical times. Similarly, in modern Eastern Orthodox and Jewish weddings, the betrothal has taken a back seat; it now occurs on the same day as the wedding ceremony.

chapter 4

bridal attendants

Since time immemorial, weddings have not been considered legitimate without witnesses. This is probably the main reason couples select attendants: bridesmaids, the maid or matron of honor, groomsmen, and the best man.

The tradition of the maid (or matron) of honor is thought to have originated in ancient Greece. In this culture, an older, happily married woman was assigned the task of escorting the young teenage bride to the wedding — perhaps imparting the secrets of marriage to her along the way. In the Middle Ages, the maid or matron of honor was there not only to support her friend and act as a witness but to testify that the bride wasn't being forced into marriage — that she was willingly going to the altar. Probably beginning in the Elizabethan era, the maid of honor also helped the bride prepare for the wedding. For example, she might make decorations for the ceremony or sew linens for the bride's new home. Traditionally, the maid or matron of honor is the bride's sister or best friend.

One of the first records of what we might now call bridesmaids can be found in the Bible. (For an example, see Psalm 45:14: "In her beautiful robes, she is led to the king, accompanied by her bridesmaids" [NLT].) Bridesmaids, too, are traditional helpers. In the past, their duties nearly always included making bouquets and wreaths for both the bride and groom. Traditionally, bridesmaids were unmarried women, and their presence during the ceremony symbolized purity.

The saying "Always a bridesmaid, never a bride" goes back to at least the sixteenth century, when it was thought that if a young woman wasn't married before her third time as a bridesmaid, her chances for marriage were slim indeed. (But the part of the saying that's forgotten today is that if she serves as a bridesmaid *seven* times, the evil spell is broken.) Traditionally, the bride's unmarried sisters took precedence as bridesmaids, followed by the groom's sisters.

The best man and groomsmen are said to date back to a time when brides were stolen. Because the bride had a family to defend her, it was necessary for the groom to have friends to help fight them off. It's said that the original reason the best man stood at the groom's side during the wedding ceremony was to keep a sharp lookout (and a hand on his sword) for anyone who might try to prevent the wedding. However, an earlier source — the Bible — mentions what we'd now call groomsmen. Here they appear not as warriors but as helpers, preparing the wedding celebration and generally supporting the groom. (For an example, see Judges 14:11, which records that Samson was given thirty companions before his wedding.)

chapter 5

bridal registries

gift registries are a modern custom. Until quite recently, creating a registry was considered too similar to asking outright for gifts — something that's not exactly polite. Today, however, gift registries of all kinds are readily accepted in the United States as a handy method of ensuring friends and family don't buy the couple twenty toasters and ten different sets of salt and pepper shakers.

The first bridal registries appeared in the early 1900s, when jewelers often sold silver goods and china in addition to jewelry. At this time, some storekeepers began jotting down a record of the couple's favorite patterns as an aid to those buying them presents.

By the late 1930s, department stores started advertising what we'd now call bridal registry services. (The Marshall Field's website proudly claims dibs on being the first department store to offer bridal registries.) The emphasis in these ads was always on preventing duplicate gifts — not on couples asking outright for things they wanted. Still, it took a few more decades for registries to catch on and gain the popularity they have today.

chapter 6

bridal showers

according to Victorian etiquette books, the first bridal shower was the result of poverty. The story goes that a certain friend of the bride couldn't afford to buy a substantial gift fully expressing the joy she felt for the bride. So she got together with the bride's other friends, and they all presented her with small tokens — the cumulative effect seeming more in keeping with their love for the bride.

Another oft-told story is that about three hundred years ago, a certain bride wished to marry a poor man — but her father wouldn't allow the marriage until the potential groom had a house that was "properly set up" for his daughter. Since the groom couldn't afford to furnish a house, the bride's friends got together and "showered" her with a pan here and a towel there until she had a well-appointed home.

Although there is probably a bit of truth in both stories, there is no way to trace the custom back to a certain bride — or even a particular era.

Traditionally, bridal shower gifts are household items meant to help the couple set up their first home. Today many couples have already established their own households; in such cases, a little imagination comes into play. (For example, from the eighteenth through the early twentieth century, when many people had more time than money, it was common for Americans to host quilting bees for newly engaged women instead of bridal showers. The resulting quilt was given to the bride to provide her with a household linen that could last a lifetime.) Today's brides-to-be may receive lingerie, pampering products, plants for the couple's new home, and other such gifts instead of household goods.

A longstanding tradition dictates that a member of the bride's family may not throw the bridal shower, because doing so might come across as self-serving. Instead, a friend (who also acts as maid of honor or bridesmaid) has the privilege. Nonetheless, these rules have been greatly relaxed today, and in many regions, it's considered acceptable for anyone to throw a shower for the bride.

chapter 7

bride price

although the bride price is sometimes confused with a dowry, in the strictest sense, the bride price refers only to gifts the groom and his family give to the bride's family. (A dowry involves gifts given by the bride's family to the bride, the groom, or his family.)

Several examples of the tradition of setting a bride price are found in the Bible. Perhaps the most gruesome example is when Saul asked David for "no other price for the bride" than evidence that he'd killed one hundred of the king's enemies (1 Sam. 18:25).

During biblical times, it was highly unusual for a younger sister to marry before an older one. Since Rachel was the younger of two unmarried sisters, Jacob offered a generous bride price in order to appeal to her father: seven years of labor (Gen. 29:15–18). Fifty shekels was considered a large bride price during biblical times, and Jacob's offer was probably worth about eighty-four shekels.

Today many people think the bride price was a way of selling women, but in the Bible it was more like a token of goodwill, meant to bring two families together. Some historians even think the bride price was a way of offsetting the expense of the wedding, which was usually paid for by the bride's family. Whatever the case, the practice of establishing a bride price is still a custom in some areas of the world, including India and parts of the Middle East.

chapter 8

bridesmaids' tea

although the tradition of the bridesmaids' tea is fairly recent, undoubtedly the spirit behind the tea has been kept for centuries. This afternoon tea or luncheon is a chance for the bride to thank her wedding-day helpers. The event typically culminates in a grand "bridesmaids' cake," which has silver- or gold-plated charms baked inside to "tell the future" of the bridesmaids and maid (or matron) of honor.

This custom dates to the nineteenth century; at that time, the most prized charm was a silver knot, symbolizing true love. A heart foretold a future romance; a cat indicated the unlucky charm-holder would be an old maid. A dime predicted wealth, a wishbone signified good luck, and a silver ring foretold a future wedding. In a variation of this tradition, a ribbon was tied to each charm, and the charm was placed atop the bottom layer of cake. This tradition is sometimes still practiced today, and plastic, metal, or silver-plated charms may be purchased at many bridal and baking-supply stores.

chapter 9

bundling

◆

I n the United Stated, bundling began in the Colonial era. When a young man and woman took a liking to each other, their parents arranged for them to "bundle," or sleep together without having sex. In some cases, a mother might prepare her daughter for bundling, then leave the bedroom window open and place a candle in it so that any fellow who saw the light might hop in through the window and bundle with the girl.

During bundling, both the man and the woman remained well dressed (either in their everyday clothes or in under- and nightclothes), and the young woman was usually sewed into a sack that covered her knees, hips, and underarms. (Sometimes instead of using a "bundling sack," a board was placed between the couple.) Sex was forbidden, as this eighteenth-century rhyme indicates:

Since in a bed a man and maid
May bundle and be chaste,
It does no good to burn out wood;
It is needless waste.

But bundling is also known to have led to some hasty wedding ceremonies.

It's possible that bundling was based in part on the biblical account of Ruth lying beside Boaz on the threshing floor. In this Old Testament story, Ruth, a young widow, was determined to use her legal right to ask her kinsman, Boaz, to marry her (see

34

Deut. 25:5–10). It was harvesting season, and after a day of gathering grain, crowds gathered to separate the kernels from the chaff. Ruth joined the festive atmosphere of Boaz's threshing-room floor to help with the work. As the evening turned dark and the crowds left, Ruth moved from the shadows to the place where Boaz had settled in to sleep for the night. She lay at his feet and moved his blanket so that it covered her. In this way, Ruth gently asked Boaz to marry her (see Ruth 3).

However, unlike this biblical account, bundling was not in any way a promise of protection or marriage, nor even necessarily a hint from the woman that she was willing to marry the man.

Some scholars think bundling came from the Netherlands, where the Dutch called it *queesten*. (In New York, bundling was sometimes called "questing," a variation on the Dutch name.) In this tradition, the woman stayed beneath the covers, while the man lay on top of them, trying to woo her. Similar traditions were sometimes practiced in Scandinavia, Germany, England, and elsewhere.

Bundling was mostly practiced in rural areas, and to the modern mind, it may seem incredibly lax for a time when premarital sex was widely considered taboo. Many sermons were written against bundling, but as late as the 1930s, bundling was still being practiced in some areas of the United States.

chapter 10

capturing the bride

♦

In pagan cultures, capturing the bride was a (less than conventional) way to obtain a wife. Whether the woman was captured during warfare, in a village raid, or merely because the man desired her but couldn't obtain permission to marry her, being stolen was — as you can imagine — rarely fun for the bride.

In ancient times, women captured during warfare surely expected to become the wives of the men who warred against their community; this scenario was common among almost all cultures. Although the idea seems cruel today (what woman wants to marry a man who killed her family?), it brought "fresh blood" to villages and probably prevented genetic diseases from cropping up among tight-knit communities. In the Old Testament, several mentions are made of "captured brides." Biblical law put limitations on what was acceptable and gave the bride rights unheard of in pagan cultures. For example, the Bible insists that captured brides be allowed time to mourn their family; it also declares it illegal to sell captured brides or treat them as slaves (Deut. 21:10–14).

Some people speculate that the modern idea of honeymoons came from the old practice of "stealing" brides. They say that after the groom stole the bride, he took her to a remote location until her family accepted the marriage. This idea is difficult to prove either true or false, but it probably has a degree of truth to it.

While many myths still exist about captured brides, such tales were so widely believed in eighteenth- and nineteenth-century England that captures were sometimes staged: the groomsmen "invaded" the bride's house while the bridesmaids feigned "protecting" the bride.

chapter II

counseling

premarital counseling is something that most pastors and priests require before they will marry a couple. How much time couples are required to devote to counseling depends on the church denomination and the minister. In some instances, premarital counseling may involve only a single one-hour session; other times a month-long, intensive program may be required. Most premarital counseling falls somewhere in between.

Formal premarital counseling began in the twentieth century — although religious leaders probably offered such services on a less formal basis during biblical times. For example, the betrothal period for the Hebrews may have acted much like today's premarital counseling; it was a time for the bride and groom to get to know each other better — no doubt discussing ideas, ambitions, and expectations.

The Roman Catholic Church began official premarital counseling (called "Pre-Cana") in 1980, although premarital counseling had been used by many priests for several decades. The Roman Catholic Church was the first to formally insist on counseling for couples wishing to marry in the church, but today most Protestant churches follow suit.

Unfortunately, many couples approach the required counseling as if it will be a chore. Few engaged couples think they need counseling, but current divorce statistics (which, in the United States, are the same for Christians and non-Christians) suggest that good premarital counseling is something no couple can afford to miss. If nothing else, couples can look forward to learning more about their future husband or wife during the sessions. Couples can also expect to discuss the meaning of Christ in their lives, their expectations for marriage, financial matters, family planning, their feelings about divorce, and related topics. It should be an enlightening time in which they hammer out any difficulties in their relationship *before* they commit to a permanent covenant.

chapter 12

dowries

For many centuries, brides have considered dowries vitally important. Fathers frequently tucked away money and treasures for their daughters, preparing for the day when a marriage contract would be signed. In ancient Greece, fathers are said to have given 10 percent of their wealth to their daughter's dowry. The biblical Hebrews viewed the dowry as an early portion of a daughter's rightful inheritance.

Although we may wince at the thought today, in many cultures, good dowries were intended to attract good husbands. Since dowries were usually considered (at least in part) the bride's property, a large dowry may have made a husband more congenial to his wife — and if the woman was widowed or her marriage went awry, she could use the dowry to live on. Nineteenth-century etiquette books make it clear that the question of a dowry should not be neglected; according to *The Habits of Good Society*, the dowry was considered a "fund which cannot be touched — a something, however small, [that is] a provision for a wife."

In some areas of the world, the dowry was proportional to the groom's financial status, thereby ensuring that a woman from a poor family could not marry a man of higher standing. The tradition of dowries still persists in some countries, but today a "bride price" is often mistakenly identified as a dowry.

chapter 13

engagement parties

the first engagement parties were probably the betrothal parties of the ancient Hebrews; after the marriage contract was signed and the groom bestowed gifts on his bride, a celebratory betrothal (or engagement) party began.

Traditionally, the engagement party is hosted by the groom's parents — although in recent generations, the planning duties are often undertaken by the bride's parents. Perhaps ideally, both sets of parents work together to make a memorable evening for all involved. (Hosting the party jointly creates an excellent opportunity for the parents to get to know each other too.) Sometimes the engagement is kept a secret; friends are gathered for an "ordinary" party or dinner, and then the engagement is suddenly announced. Traditionally, the father of the bride does the honors.

It's rare for engaged couples to receive gifts at this time. (There is, however, an old tradition of giving teacups as engagement presents. The story accompanying this tradition involves a sailor who departed for an extended trip; before leaving, he gave his bride-to-be a china teacup and asked her to drink from it daily, saying, "If I am unfaithful, the cup will fill to overflowing, and the tea pouring over the sides will crack the china." The story is almost certainly mythical.) However, if the couple is given engagement gifts, they should be opened after the party so guests who didn't bring gifts won't feel bad.

Following the engagement party, it was common for friends of eighteenth- and nineteenth-century couples to host dinners or balls in honor of the prospective bride and groom.

chapter 14

engagement rings

Since ancient times, engagement or betrothal rings have been used to show good faith. Giving his intended a valuable ring was one way for the groom to assure the bride and her family that he was going to "make good" on his promise to marry her.

Early rings were made from plain gold or iron. The wealthy used gemstone rings, and the Romans sometimes attached their house keys to rings as an expression of how much they trusted their fiancées.

In the eighth century, fancy engagement rings came into fashion; some featured three-dimensional mini-temples, while others included jeweled boxes that could hold small treasures. In AD 860, Pope Nicholas decreed a gold ring a requirement of engagement; he wanted to ensure that engagements wouldn't be made lightly, with no real intention of marriage. Before this time, it was mostly those who were well off who participated in the engagement ring tradition.

By the fifteenth century, diamonds were used extensively in the engagement rings of the wealthy; they were intended to impress the bride's family and fellow townspeople. Diamonds were known to be the most enduring precious stone; therefore, they seemed a fitting symbol for a marriage that would last forever. It wasn't until the 1870s that the diamond solitaire engagement ring, created by the famous jeweler Tiffany, came into vogue. (The idea behind diamond engagement rings probably comes from pagan mythology. Cupid's arrows — which were said to make people fall in love — were supposedly diamond-tipped.)

Throughout the Victorian era, "regard" rings also were popular for engagements. The first letter of each gemstone used spelled out the bride's name, the word *love*, or some other pertinent word. For example, the word *dear* was "spelled" with a *d*iamond, *e*merald, *a*methyst, and *r*uby.

In the 1920s, jewelers made an unsuccessful bid at selling male engagement rings. Although their ads tried to convince couples that men had worn engagement rings for centuries, brides and grooms didn't buy it. There is some indication, however, that male engagement rings were occasionally worn in the early nineteenth century; today engagement rings for men are fairly common in some countries.

Throughout history, engagement rings with faux stones have been taboo, as they seem to symbolize false intentions. For those who couldn't afford a gemstone ring, plain gold bands, sometimes engraved with the date of engagement, were often given; later they doubled as the wedding band.

Just as in times past, today's engagement rings are not mandatory. Still, many grooms want to give their bride something as a symbol of their promise, faith, and love. Whether the groom buys the ring before he proposes is entirely up to him; while having the ring handy when he's on one knee is traditional and romantic, some brides prefer to help pick out the ring that will rest on their finger for the rest of their lives.

Today's couples shouldn't feel obliged to pick a diamond. An engagement ring may have any sort of stone desired. Many brides are just as happy with a ring that features their birth-stone, their fiancé's birthstone, or a combination of the two. Sometimes the stone representing the month a couple will marry is chosen. And some rings have no stones at all but are attractively designed entirely of gold or silver.

For those who love lore and history, gem symbolism may be a consideration. Most of the well-known symbolic meanings behind gemstones come from pagan stories, but the Bible refers to some gems, and Hebrew and early Christian cultures also attached meanings to particular stones. If you're wary of using birthstones because you think they're linked with astrology, you should know that many scholars believe the idea of having a stone represent your birth comes from the breastpiece of Israel (Exod. 28:15–30), on which each Hebrew tribe was represented by a different stone.

In Anglo and Hebrew tradition, the **garnet** is the stone of January. The stone's modern name comes from the ancient Greeks, who thought it resembled a *Punica granatum*, or pome-granate seed. According to the Talmud (an ancient Jewish commentary on the Old Testament), Noah hung a huge, brilliant garnet on his ark and used it as a lamp. In addition, the deep red color of the garnet has traditionally suggested devotion and loyalty.

The **amethyst** is traditionally February's stone in both Anglo and Hebrew history. Its shade is purple, the color of royalty — which combines the colors red (symbolizing passion) and blue (symbolizing heaven). When God gave instructions for building his temple and its contents, the amethyst was among the stones mounted on the "breastpiece for making decisions" (Exod. 28:15, 19). The amethyst stood for the tribe of Gad, who "carried out the LORD's righteous will" (Deut. 33:21).

In Anglo tradition, the **aquamarine** is March's stone. With its light blue color, it has come to be associated with youth, hope, health, the heavens, and the ocean. (The word *aquamarine* means seawater.) The Hebrews used **bloodstone** as March's birthstone, which later came to symbolize Christ's purifying blood.

The **diamond** is traditionally April's stone in Anglo history. In some translations of the Bible (such as the King James Version and the New American Standard Bible), a diamond appears on the Israelites' breastpiece to represent the house of Dan (Exod. 28:18). The beginning of that tribe was Rachel's son Dan, about whom Rachel said, "God has vindicated me" (Gen. 30:6). In some translations, the diamond is also mentioned as a stone found in the garden of Eden (Ezek. 28:13). Because of diamonds' hardness and durability, they are generally associated with eternity. The ancient Hebrews regarded the **sapphire** as March's birthstone.

The **emerald** is traditionally May's stone, although the Hebrews preferred **agate**. Because of their vivid, springlike green color, emeralds are generally associated with rebirth and fertility. When the Israelites' breastpiece was made, the emerald on it symbolized the house of Zebulun, whose name meant "honor" (Gen. 30:20). The emerald is also mentioned in the Bible as one of the stones found in Eden (Ezek. 28:13). In ancient times, emeralds were mined near the Red Sea.

The **pearl** or **agate** is June's stone in Anglo tradition. An agate was mounted on the Israelites' breastpiece to symbolize the tribe of Naphtali, who was "abounding with the favor of the LORD and is full of his blessing" (Deut. 33:23). The pearl often represents new life or rebirth because it comes from (or is given birth to by) a living creature — an oyster. The ancient Hebrews designated the **emerald** as June's stone.

The **ruby** is traditionally July's stone; the Hebrews used **onyx** instead. The ancients called the ruby the "king of gems," and its red color associates it with passion, love, and fire. In the

Old Testament, a ruby was mounted on the Israelites' breast-piece to symbolize the house of Reuben; the tribe is named after Leah's son Reuben, who brought her mandrakes in order to help her win the love of her husband (Gen. 30:14). The ruby is also listed as one of the gems found in Eden (Ezek. 28:13). Onyx is associated with the number seven, the biblical number of perfection or completion.

The **peridot** is traditionally August's stone in the Anglo world; the ancient Hebrews preferred **carnelian**. Peridots have been mined in the Red Sea for over 3,500 years. Before chemical classification of stones was invented, peridots were thought to be emeralds. (In fact, all red gemstones were called rubies, and all green gemstones were called emeralds.) Carnelian was symbolic of God's seal; this stone was widely used for covenant seals of all kinds because it was thought not to stick to wax.

In Anglo history, the **sapphire** is traditionally September's stone (the Hebrews used the **peridot** instead). In times past, some people believed that the heavens crystallized and formed a huge sapphire for the earth to sit on. This idea may have come from the book of Exodus, in which Moses sees God standing on "something like a pavement made of sapphire" (Exod. 24:10). Two similar passages, describing God's "throne of sapphire," appear in Ezekiel (1:26; 10:1). The ancient Jews also believed that the Ten Commandments were written on a tablet of sapphire. Sapphires have long been associated with heaven and truth. A sapphire was included on the Israelites' breastpiece to symbolize the house of Issachar; this tribe was named after Leah's son Issachar, whose name sounded like the Hebrew word for "reward" (Gen. 30:18). Sapphires are also cited as having been in the garden of Eden (Ezek. 28:13).

The **opal** is traditionally October's stone, although the Hebrews designated the **aquamarine** for this month. In some translations of the Bible, an opal appears on the Israelites'

breastpiece to symbolize the house of Dan. The opal traditionally symbolizes hope. Because of the many fragmented colors
found in opals, they were once thought to be bits of rainbows
that had fallen to the ground.

The **topaz** is traditionally November's stone in both Anglo
and Hebrew history. A topaz was mounted on the Israelites'
breastpiece to represent the house of Simeon (Exod. 28:17);
this tribe was named for Leah's son Simeon, whose name
meant "the One who hears" (Gen. 29:33). The topaz is also
found among the listed gems of Eden (Ezek. 28:13). The word
topaz is thought to come from the island of Topazos in the Red
Sea, where topaz was often discovered.

Turquoise or **blue topaz** is traditionally December's stone
in Anglo history, but the Hebrews used the **ruby**. Turquoise was
mounted on Israel's breastpiece to represent the tribe of Judah
(Exod. 28:18); this tribe was named for Leah's son Judah,
whose name probably meant "praise" (Gen. 29:35). Turquoise
is also named as a stone found in Eden (Ezek. 28:13), and it
is mentioned as having been used in the temple Solomon built
(1 Chron. 29:2). Turquoise was traditionally thought to have
originated in the wet ground at the end of a rainbow.

chapter 15

Flower girls, pages, and ring bearers

the flower girl probably originated in biblical times, when children frequently led the bridal group to the location of the wedding ceremony; in some cultures, these children threw herbs and grains on the bride's path as a token to the pagan gods. In the medieval era, two young girls often walked to the ceremony holding wheat — a pagan symbol for fertility. In the Elizabethan era, when flower cultivation became popular, the girls began carrying and wearing blooms; floral wreaths, symbolizing innocence, often adorned their heads. Today some churches don't allow the strewing of flowers because of the damage it can cause to flooring, but flower girls may still carry and wear flowers.

Pages are believed to have been added to wedding ceremonies in the medieval era; their role was to hold excessively long bridal trains. This idea was probably borrowed from the royal courts, where young boys often held queens' trains.

Although one might wonder why a ring bearer is necessary at all, assigning a person solely to the task of holding the wedding bands shows just how important the concept of rings was thought to be. Going back to ancient times, ring bearers kept the wedding bands on a special pillow, but in the Victorian era, many creative ring holders were used — including calla lily blooms. Ring bearers haven't always been boys, either. In the Victorian era, girls often held the rings, and in ancient times, an adult of either sex might have had the honor.

invitations

In biblical times, written invitations didn't exist. Instead, invitations were given to the entire community by word of mouth.

The first printed invitations were used by wealthy families in the Middle Ages. These handwritten invitations were made by monks and were probably inspired by the monasteries' careful record keeping of the marriages of nobility. By the seventeenth century, engraved cards were possible, making invitations available to a wider group of people. Still, simple invitations were considered best, and Victorian etiquette books abound with warnings against purchasing "fancy paper or type."

In all cases, the invitations had to be hand delivered; there were no post offices then. Even in the nineteenth century, when the post office was fairly well established, many people preferred the more personal method of hand delivery.

No one knows for sure when the tradition of using two envelopes started. Etiquette books from the 1920s suggest that the innermost envelope (which, they say, should remain unsealed) is used to protect the card from damage, while the outer envelope is meant to be marked up for mailing. Given that wedding invitations are often the most costly and fancy cards a person will ever use, this added protection makes sense. Even though printed invitations have been favored, throughout the years, whenever a couple has longed for a small, low-key wedding, informal letters have usually been sent instead.

While modern brides may find the small, separate card inviting guests to the reception wasteful, its origins probably date to the Victorian era, when large church weddings were fashionable but receptions were usually held at private homes. Since hundreds of people couldn't fit into the average house, only a fraction of the guests were invited to the reception. The addition of a small card with the invitation made it possible to customize invitations easily.

The rectangles of tissue still included with most traditional invitations also date back to the eighteenth and nineteenth century; they were included to prevent slow-drying ink from smearing.

chapter 17

location and time

In biblical days, the Hebrews typically held wedding ceremonies at the bride's home. The ancient Greeks also favored home ceremonies, usually conducting the wedding in front of the home hearth, where they made sacrifices to their gods. Early Christians often held their ceremonies on the church steps and only much later began holding weddings inside the church. In the American colonies, at-home weddings were common because of the Puritan Civil Marriage Act, which stated that only marriages made by the justice of the peace were legal. This law didn't last long, but it imbued a tradition of home weddings in the American heart.

No one knows for certain why most weddings were eventually held in churches. It is true that over time churches also became community centers; it wasn't uncommon for towns to hold *all* of their important community events at the church — and weddings were certainly no exception.

Throughout history, many superstitions have surrounded the "correct" time to marry. For example, an old English verse declares:

Married when the year is new,
He'll be loving, kind, and true.
When February birds do mate,
You wed, or dread your fate.
If you wed when March winds blow,

Joy and sorrow both you'll know.
Marry in April if you can,
Joy for maiden and for man.
Marry in the month of May,
And you'll surely rue the day.
Marry when June roses grow,
O'er land and sea you'll go.
Those who in July do wed,
Must labor for their daily bread.
Whoever wed in August be
Many a change is sure to see.
Marry in September's shine,
Your living will be rich and fine.
If in October you do marry,
Love will come, but riches tarry.
If you wed in bleak November,
Only joys will come, remember.
When December's snow falls fast,
Marry, and true love will last.

The ancient Greeks believed January was the ideal wedding month because it was dedicated to Hera (Zeus's wife and the advocate of women). The ancient Romans held fertility rites in January, adding to the month's appeal. Later, after these pagan ideas were mostly forgotten, the first month of the year was considered a good month to start any new endeavor — including marriage.

When Christians began practicing Lent (probably around the fourth century), the forty days of that season became a time to avoid weddings. This tradition died out in the nineteenth century, soon after Queen Victoria (who was the titular head of the Church of England) declared marriage "a solemn holy act, not to be classed with amusements," and insisted that her eldest son be married during Lent. Among the ancient Romans, March (named for Mars, the pagan god of war) was considered a bad time to marry; who wants to associate marriage with war?

Since ancient times, April has been considered a good month to marry because it was the month of Venus, the Roman goddess of love. More practically, many rural communities favored March because it fell shortly before harvesting and planting; after March there would be little time for weddings. The ancient Romans avoided May because the Feast of the Dead fell during this month.

June is still the most popular month for weddings, partly because of the many engagements that take place during the Christmas season but also because the notion of a "June bride" is still prevalent in our society. The origin of June brides goes back to the ancient Romans, who enjoyed weddings in June because it was the month of Juno (a goddess thought to protect women). In addition, June may have been chosen for more practical reasons: roses — the traditional wedding decoration — are abundant during this month.

July was a less popular month for marriage; in rural areas, this was when preparations were made for harvesting. Similarly, August was rarely chosen in rural areas because it was the first month of harvesting.

The ancients believed that September's full harvest moon symbolized fertility, making it a popular marriage month. The ancient Greeks preferred cold-weather weddings in October and November.

Days of the week also have their superstitions. A popular rhyme gave details:

Monday for wealth,
Tuesday for health,
Wednesday is the best day of all,

Thursday for losses,
Friday for crosses,
Saturday, no luck at all.

Today, for practical reasons, most weddings are held on the weekend; it's more difficult for friends and family to attend a wedding if they must take time off work. Sunday weddings have generally been shunned by Christians because Sunday is the Sabbath. (For Christians who maintain the Old Testament custom of a Saturday Sabbath, Sunday is the preferred weekend day for weddings.)

Traditionally, most cultures have preferred morning weddings, often followed by a religious service. Morning weddings make a lot of sense: the ceremony and reception are exhausting and time-consuming, and an evening wedding makes for a very late night. Nonetheless, royalty has often favored evening ceremonies; the Bible also mentions weddings held at night (see Matt. 25:1, for example).

Even the weather on the day of the wedding carries some folklore along with it. Old-time wisdom says that if it's sunny, the couple will spend all their days happily. If it snows, they'll have wealth; and if it rains, their marriage will be tear-free.

chapter 18

marriage contracts

◆

In the past, the idea that marriage was a covenant or contract was readily acknowledged. In ancient times, a marriage or betrothal contract was frequently made — but was often little more than a list of properties to be exchanged. However, the Hebrews developed a much more meaningful contract, called the *ketubah* (which literally means "her writing"). This contract was read aloud at the betrothal ceremony and was prepared by the groom. In it, the husband-to-be detailed his responsibilities to his future wife. Typically the *ketubah* outlined the groom's promise to feed, clothe, and shelter his wife; respect and honor her; not make her cry; and serve her to the best of his abilities.

The oldest *ketubah* archeologists have found dates to the third century BC; this early date makes it an especially amazing artifact since most surrounding societies of the same time period treated women like chattels.

Early Christians had their own form of the *ketubah* but added to it the wife's promise to "love, cherish, and honor" her husband. Today Christian couples are once again exploring the tradition of the *ketubah*, or written marriage covenant. Specially printed, decorative versions of the *ketubah* can be found in Christian and Jewish bookstores, but some couples prefer to create a simple, handwritten document that can be framed or rolled up and tied with ribbons for safekeeping. By writing out their sacred promises to each other and signing and witnessing the document, couples are not only creating a cherished heirloom, they are making it clear where the focus of their marriage will be: on serving God and each other.

chapter 19

parents' dinner

the parents' dinner is a modern tradition, started by couples who became engaged without asking parental permission. The get-together has a twofold design: to announce the engagement to both sets of parents and to let the families get to know each other, if they don't already. Traditionally, the groom's parents host the dinner, but it's increasingly common for the dinner to be held at the bride's parents' home or at a restaurant.

chapter 20

promise rings

The origins of what we call "promise rings" date to ancient times, when betrothals were an important marriage custom. Many betrothal ceremonies required the soon-to-be groom to show good faith by giving his intended a betrothal ring; it was a symbol of his promise to marry her, although the wedding might take place months — even years — later.

The term *promise ring* (and the idea behind it) was established about a decade ago. The giving of this ring is a custom followed mostly by Christians and is a way for young couples to promise that someday (typically at no set date) they will marry. A promise ring usually assumes the marriage will take place more than a year after the time of giving; it comes before the engagement ring, which is given when the couple is ready to begin planning their wedding.

proposals

Originally, in almost all cultures, marriages were arranged by parents. The man didn't pop the question to the woman; one father popped the question to another father. But as a more romantic view of marriage began to take hold, it wasn't uncommon for a potential groom to ask permission of his intended's father — sometimes without asking the bride first. Later, letter writing was the favored way for a gentleman to propose to a lady; once the man knew the woman was favorable to the idea of marriage, he asked her father for permission. By the 1920s, however, the tradition of asking the father's permission began dying out. The custom isn't entirely dead, though. Tradition-loving grooms still sometimes ask their girlfriend's father for permission to marry her.

It's thought that the tradition of proposing while on bended knee dates back to the days of knights, when this position was one servants took in front of their mistresses. Knights also went down on bended knee before jousting tournaments, asking for their lady's favor in the form of a handkerchief or scarf.

Although we tend to think of women proposing to men as a modern custom, as early as 1900 the idea was seriously being discussed in etiquette books. In addition, the Bible gave Hebrew widows the right to insist a kinsman to marry them. (See Matthew 22:24: "Moses told us that if a man dies without having children, his brother must marry the widow and have children for him.") Acting on this right, Ruth asked her kinsman Boaz to marry her (see Ruth 3:9). In addition, women of high rank almost always had the privilege of proposing marriage. In fact, no one was allowed to propose to a queen — *she* had to do the proposing.

For hundreds of years it has also been considered acceptable for women to propose on February 29, during leap year. Originally leap day wasn't recognized by English law; because of this lack of legal status, it seemed a good day to break with tradition. This custom may go as far back as the fifth century, when St. Bridget is said to have complained to St. Patrick that women had to wait too long for men to propose marriage. According to this legend, St. Patrick gave his approval for women to do the proposing on leap day. In 1288, Scotland passed a law allowing women to propose on leap day — and any man who refused the proposal had to pay a fine. This fine could entail anything from kissing the woman to buying her a new dress.

chapter 22

transportation to the ceremony

traveling to the site of the wedding has always been a big event. In biblical days, the groom usually walked to the bride's home, accompanied by friends and family. Traditionally, music and dancing were an important part of this journey.

Later, when weddings were held at churches, both the bride and groom walked to the site with their family and friends. Although it's probable the crowds helped prevent last-minute cold feet, some historians suggest superstitious families led the couple to the church in hopes of keeping evil spells at bay. In ancient Greece, brides were usually accompanied by ten female friends who carried lanterns to help ward off evil spirits. The Bible also mentions what we'd now call bridesmaids, carrying oil lamps (Matt. 25: 1).

While we tend to think the idea of traveling to the ceremony in a white limo (or for the more romantic, a horse-drawn carriage) is a modern idea, it probably dates to an old German custom of the bride arriving at the church in a white carriage. In fact, brides often arrived in splendor; Hebrew brides sometimes rode to the wedding ceremony in a fancy litter, Turkish brides rode beneath a canopy mounted on a horse, and ancient Chinese brides rode in a sedan chair. While it may be true that some people believed this special mode of transportation prevented evil spirits (thought to live just under the soil) from noticing the bride, surely one reason behind this tradition stems from the idea of the bride being "queen for a day."

trousseaux and hope chests

Some form of the trousseau probably has existed since ancient times. Indeed, it's likely that during biblical times, brides' dowries included a trousseau of household goods and clothing.

Originally the trousseau was a practical matter. The groom provided a home, but the bride was expected to supply the many details of everyday life: linens, cookware, and such. The word *trousseau* comes from a French word meaning "bundle" and brings to mind a time when the trousseau arrived at the couple's home on a donkey's back.

Women who weren't wealthy often kept a "hope chest," a tradition that still survives today. The hope chest is a container of some sort that gradually gets filled with items for the bridal trousseau. A hope chest might be started by a mother when her daughter is still an infant, or the daughter might start it later, when she's old enough to make or buy the items to go in it. After marriage, the hope chest becomes a place to store the wedding gown, baby clothes, and any other heirlooms the bride might wish to pass down to her children.

The bride of old needed not just household items in her trousseau but also fashion items. She tried to provide enough underclothes for most of her life and enough dresses to clothe herself for many years; all items were of the finest quality the bride's family could afford. Victorian brides had some of the most lavish trousseaux ever known. When Florence Adele

Sloane (a Vanderbilt niece) married an English lord in 1895, her trousseau included duplicate gowns for every imaginable social function and reputedly cost $40,000. That's a pretty substantial sum today — but in the late nineteenth century, it equaled seventy years' wages for the average man. According to writers of the era, a modest trousseau contained three dozen of everything.

One of the more bizarre rituals surrounding the trousseau was putting it on public display. An average bride might display her trousseau in the family parlor during a small party with close friends and family, but a wealthy bride often had her trousseau set up in a more showy fashion, displayed to hundreds of guests. While some people felt that displaying the bride's trousseau (complete with underwear) was in poor taste, the practice continued through the early 1900s.

The beginning of the twentieth century was also when trousseaux declined in size and extravagance. Fashions now changed too rapidly for brides to include much in the way of clothing, and the focus was given back to household items such as linens, washtubs, and pans. Today few brides have a formal trousseau — unless they've kept a hope chest. Most modern trousseaux are wardrobes of lingerie.

part 2

ceremony traditions

aisle runners

the white aisle runner dates to ancient Hebrew custom and represents walking on holy ground. It's also a reminder that God is present during both the ceremony and the marriage — and that marriage is not just between two people but three: husband, wife, and God.

Although some people assume the red aisle runner is a modern wedding innovation, mimicking the "red carpet" of fairy tales and Hollywood award ceremonies, red aisle runners actually go back many centuries. Originally, they were used to ward off evil spirits who might linger on the ground.

chapter 25

bridal accessories

The Veil

Since biblical times, brides have worn veils; but depending on the bride's religion, veils have represented many different things. In Judeo-Christian cultures, the bridal veil is a symbol of purity and goes at least as far back as Jacob's marriage to Leah (which explains why he didn't recognize his bride until he woke up the following morning; see Gen. 29:22–25).

In traditional Jewish ceremonies, the groom (escorted by his soon-to-be father-in-law) covers the bride with a veil before the ceremony. To all present, the veil is a reminder of the ideals women should strive for, including chastity and dignity. It's also a reminder that inner beauty is of far more consequence than outer beauty and that physical intimacy should only take place after marriage. Early Christians adopted the bridal veil from Jewish tradition.

White bridal veils were not the norm until recent generations. During the Renaissance, for example, any color might be worn; blue, widely recognized as a symbol of purity, was often favored by Christians. The ancient Greeks preferred veils of red and flaming yellows, which represented humbleness before Hymen, the god of marriage. After the wedding ceremony, Greek brides offered their veils as a gift to Hera, the goddess of marriage, who was supposed to protect women and ensure safe childbirth.

No one is exactly sure when the tradition of lifting the bridal veil during the wedding ceremony began, but some speculate it dates at least to the medieval era. When the bridal party walked to the ceremony, the bride and her attendants traveled under a canopy, signifying that the bride was still under her father's care. When the ceremony was complete, the bride walked out from under it — showing that she was no longer part of her father's house. Somewhere along the line, the canopy disappeared, and instead, the bride's veil was lifted at the ceremony's end.

To show off wealth, lace was sometimes used instead of tulle (or semi-transparent cloth). Lace, which could only be made by hand until the mid-nineteenth century, was considered a treasure and was passed down from generation to generation as an inheritance. Therefore, until less expensive machine-made lace became available, only the wealthiest brides wore lace veils.

Tiaras, used to hold bridal veils in place, are also a long-standing tradition, dating to wealthy weddings in ancient times. Ancient Hebrew brides were crowned with floral wreaths. Later, crowns were reserved for married women; they were not supposed to be worn by maidens. Today this tradition is some-times still acknowledged, as when Sarah Ferguson wed Prince Andrew at Westminster Abby in 1986; the bride walked up the aisle wearing a wreath of flowers in her hair and came back down the aisle as a princess wearing a tiara.

Modern brides have a wide variety of veils to choose from. Most are made of tulle but can be attached to almost anything — from a modest hair comb to an elaborately jeweled crown. Today's bride may also choose to cover her face for the ceremony (a tradition that dates back to biblical times) or allow the guests to see her face throughout the entire ceremony (a practice that probably dates to the nineteenth century); either fashion reflects the heritage of the bridal veil.

Handkerchiefs

Hankies have been part of bridal wear for centuries; after all, they give the bride something to dab her eyes with during an emotional ceremony. In fact, at one time, a few tears from the bride may have been encouraged. There's an old saying that tears shed before the wedding's completion mean none after it — a sweet, if idealistic, sentiment.

Traditionally, the handkerchief is a gift to the bride and is embroidered with a monogram or the bride and groom's names. However, in superstitious Victorian times, no linens — including the bride's handkerchief — were embroidered with anything but the bride's maiden name or initials; using the bride's married name was thought presumptuous since the marriage hadn't actually taken place yet.

The hanky is often kept in the bride's sleeve but may be tucked into her purse or skirt pocket. After the ceremony, such handkerchiefs become cherished heirlooms, and many a modern bride frames her hanky for display — until her own daughter can carry it during *her* wedding.

There's another tradition about the afterlife of bridal hankies; in this nineteenth-century custom, the handkerchief is folded and ribbon ties are added, turning it into a bonnet for the bride's first baby.

Something Old, Something New …

Something old,
Something new,
Something borrowed,
Something blue,
And a silver sixpence in your shoe.

This familiar saying dates to at least the 1300s, and there is a lot of speculation about just what it means.

The "something old" is generally thought to symbolize the bride's old life; the "something new," her new life with her husband. The "something borrowed" reminds the couple that they won't have to face the world alone — they'll have support from their friends and family. The "something blue" may harken back to biblical times, when blue was the symbol of purity and fidelity.

Some scholars give more superstitious reasons for the rhyme. The "something old," they say, refers to the idea that wearing some happy item of your ancestor's will supernaturally give you the same happiness. "Something new" goes back to the idea that it's good to begin a household with new items, or you might have bad luck. "Something borrowed" again refers to the idea that if you wear something belonging to a happily married woman, you too will be happy.

The last part of the rhyme ("and a silver sixpence in your shoe," sometimes rephrased in the United States as "and a shiny penny in your shoe") is thought to come from the practices of ancient Greece, where brides carried three silver coins on their wedding day to ensure prosperity. The bride gave one coin to her mother-in-law and one coin to the first person she met on the road after the ceremony; she kept the last coin to carry into her new home.

chapter 26

bridal gowns

Special clothing has long been a part of religious ceremony. Ancient Hebrew priests wore distinctive robes during worship (see Exod. 28:4, where God explains what priests should wear), and Jewish brides took special care to adorn themselves on their wedding day. (For example, Psalm 45:13–14 says, "The bride, a princess, waits within her chamber, dressed in a gown woven with gold. In her beautiful robes, she is led to the king, accompanied by her bridesmaids" [NLT]; and Isaiah 49:18 says, "'As surely as I live,' declares the LORD, 'you will wear them all as ornaments; you will put them on, like a bride.") But while bridal gowns are an old and cherished custom, perhaps no other wedding tradition is so misunderstood.

The most common misconception about bridal gowns is that they have always been white to symbolize virginity. Yet up until fairly recent times, most wedding gowns were *not* white.

Before clothing could be dropped off at the dry cleaner's, white was the most impractical of all colors. It soiled easily and was difficult to clean. Therefore, a nonwashable white gown wasn't useful for any length of time ... and our ancestors were eminently more practical than we are today. Unless they were quite wealthy, they couldn't imagine buying a gown to wear once or twice. Therefore, most brides wore colored dresses that could easily be used for future events.

Historians tell us that during biblical times, many brides and grooms chose to wear their best clothes accessorized with a blue sash — which symbolized purity. Later, blues and purples were popular among the wedding attire of the wealthy, and in the eighteenth century, yellow was the craze for a while. During the American Revolution, some brides showed their patriotism by donning red bridal gowns. In the Victorian era, practical navy blue, grays, and browns were popular choices. During the Civil War, some American brides chose to wear purple, a color used in remembrance of the wounded and killed. Colors worn by brides also varied from country to country; for example, in Spain, Roman Catholic brides often wore black lace bridal gowns.

Nobody really knows who wore the first white bridal gown, but we do know that ancient Greeks considered white symbolic of joy and youth, and their brides frequently donned white clothing. Ancient Romans also preferred white gowns — because they were the color of Hymen, the god of marriage.

The first fashion drawing of a white wedding gown appeared in 1813, but it wasn't until 1840, when England's Queen Victoria was wed, that white bridal gowns became *the* thing every woman wished to wear. The Queen's gown was an extremely elaborate affair but was quite different from typical queenly wedding attire. Instead of heavy robes overly trimmed with bulky furs and ostentatious jewels, Queen Victoria's gown dripped with lace and femininity.

Nonetheless, it wasn't every day that a queen got married, and the gown was definitely designed to impress. That's one important reason Queen Victoria chose to wear impractical white. Even that oh-so-feminine lace was designed to impress; it took two hundred sequestered needlewomen eight months to create. The end result was an elaborate gown with an eighteen-foot train, worn with a white lace veil trimmed with orange blossoms.

By the mid-nineteenth century, white gowns were considered the only thing to wear in a church wedding — and even brides married at home preferred a white dress. By the 1940s, white wedding gowns were so dear to women's hearts that Americans sent English brides (who couldn't get their hands on white cloth due to World War II) white bridal fabrics and dresses as an act of charity.

Was white chosen because it represents virginity? It's not likely, since all brides prior to the late twentieth century were assumed to be virgins anyway. The use of white was much more about being extravagant on a day of celebration. Probably the reason many people came to think of white as a symbol of virginity is this: historically, widows who were remarrying were encouraged *not* to wear white. However, this had everything to do with age — not sexual status. Older, never-before-married brides were also discouraged from wearing white, even when it was expected they were virgins.

Tellingly, white was also a common color for other dresses signifying a change in status: christening, communion, baptism, debutante, and graduation gowns were all traditionally white in the nineteenth and early twentieth centuries. In addition, until the early twentieth century, bridesmaids also frequently wore white dresses.

Yet while colors may have varied and styles fluctuated, what all traditional bridal gowns did have in common was modesty. Until recent years, it was rare to see a low-cut bridal gown, and long sleeves (or at least long gloves) were the norm.

Today, brides have a myriad of styles to choose from. Whether it's sleek and modern or full-skirted and fancy, the choice largely depends on the personality of the bride. And while it's not exactly common to consult the groom on such issues, the wise bride may want to get an idea of how her future husband feels about the subject of bridal gowns. Case in point: When I was shopping for my own bridal gown, I had trouble finding exactly the style I desired. The closest thing to perfection turned out to be a beautiful tulle affair — which was cream-colored. I ultimately chose to go with something else because I wanted a pure white gown. (I figured I'd earned what most people consider the virginal look.) After we were married, I told my husband about my bridal gown shopping adventure — and discovered he would have been disappointed if I'd worn anything other than white. He too figured we'd earned that pure-white look!

It's also traditional for the bride to save her wedding gown — both for sentiment and so that her daughter(s) might wear it. Some scholars think this tradition goes all the way back to New Testament times.

If you want to continue this tradition, there are several important details to consider. First, be certain to have the gown dry-cleaned right away — even if it looks fine. Perspiration stains, in particular, have a way of popping up unexpectedly if the dress sits without being cleaned. Even though the gown will come back from the cleaner's in a plastic bag, don't store the dress this way; fabric must breathe, or it will deteriorate. It's definitely better not to hang the dress; the weight of the fabric will eventually cause thinning and rips. Instead, store the gown flat. The box that holds the dress should be either acid-free or lined with several layers of acid-free tissue; this will prevent yellow spots from appearing on the fabric. Folds made in the dress should be stuffed with acid-free tissue to prevent permanent creases. Acid-free tissue can be found through some bridal gown stores, art supply shops, or preservation mail-order catalogs and should be replaced every few years.

chapter 27

communion

aking communion before or during the wedding ceremony may date as far back as the early Christian era. The first communion occurred at the Last Supper, just before Jesus was sent to the cross. In 1 Corinthians 11:23–26, the Bible describes this event: "The Lord Jesus, on the night he was betrayed, took bread, and when he had given thanks, he broke it and said, 'This is my body, which is for you; do this in remembrance of me.' In the same way, after supper he took the cup, saying, 'This cup is the new covenant in my blood; do this, whenever you drink it, in remembrance of me.' For whenever you eat this bread and drink this cup, you proclaim the Lord's death until he comes." Communion, then, is meant to be a reminder and a symbol of our faith.

Christian couples are not generally required to take communion during their wedding ceremony; some churches even discourage it unless communion may be taken by all in attendance. Yet when the bride and groom take communion during the ceremony, it's a wonderful reminder that they are making a covenant not just with each other but also with God.

If you're interested in taking communion during your ceremony, be sure to discuss it with your minister. If you cannot take communion during the wedding, you might consider taking it just before the ceremony. If you don't want your groom to see you before the ceremony, you might be able to take communion one-on-one with your minister.

chapter 28

electronic weddings

O n this Net, I thee wed." That's right; there are thousands of Internet sites that will marry couples these days. Just enter the bride's and groom's names, key in the vows (trying to avoid typos), click the button that says, "I do," and print out a "wedding certificate." This in no way makes for a legal marriage, but some technology-minded couples enjoy adding this new custom to their wedding experience.

In addition, weddings by webcam, in which the bride and groom are in separate cities (or states, or countries) and say their vows via live Internet video, have grown increasingly popular since the 1990s. Other couples marry the traditional way but in full view of a webcam that allows long-distance friends and relatives to be guests.

While electronic weddings might appear to be a modern custom, they actually date to the nineteenth century. During the heyday of telegraphs, male and female telegraph operators often met "online" and became romantic. According to operators of the period, many such romances culminated in marriage — some of them electronic.

Historians think the earliest electronic wedding was held in 1848. The bride was the daughter of a well-to-do Boston merchant, and the groom was the merchant's clerk. Unfortunately, the merchant disapproved of the couple's engagement and sent his clerk to England on a long business trip. Not one to have her plans thwarted, the bride-to-be telegraphed her fiancé and asked him to have a magistrate at a certain telegraph office at a particular hour. Through Morse code, the merchant's plan to marry his daughter to a man of *his* choosing was foiled — and the rich young lady and the lowly clerk were wed.

At least one other wedding took place via telegraph. In 1876, a telegraph operator at Camp Grant, Arizona, couldn't obtain a leave of absence to marry his fiancée; there was no minister at the camp, so they couldn't marry there either. The situation seemed hopeless. Then the young operator had a brilliant thought; contracts by telegraph were legally binding ... so why wouldn't a marriage by telegraph be? His fiancée traveled to Camp Grant, and a minister "attended" the marriage via telegraph machine. The father of the bride also was 650 miles away but gave his daughter in marriage through electronic tappings.

chapter 29

flowers

Orange Blossoms

Throughout history, orange blossoms have persistently been associated with brides. For example, Greek mythology explains that at Zeus and Hera's wedding, the goddess Gaea gave the bride orange blossoms on her wedding night. In Roman mythology, Juno, the goddess of women and marriage, also received orange blossoms when she married.

Somehow a similar tradition arose in China, where orange blossoms are considered symbols of fruitfulness (orange trees produce both blooms and fruit at the same time), everlasting love (the trees are evergreen), and purity. In short, orange blossoms are the Chinese bride's good luck charm. Legend has it that the European world became acquainted with the orange-blossom tradition around the time of the Crusades. By the eighteenth century, the custom was so common that the saying "to gather orange blossoms" was commonly known to mean "to get a wife."

Because many brides didn't have access to live orange blossoms, imitations became popular. They were made of paper, silk, wax, and (later) plastic; custom said they shouldn't be thrown away until the length of time passed that real orange blossoms would have withered.

Myrtle

Ancient Greek religion includes a story about how Aph-
rodite, the goddess of love, emerged from the ocean carrying
wreaths of myrtle; and indeed, it's easy to see why the ancients
associated myrtle with love and marriage. The plant is evergreen
and can bloom year-round — ideal symbols of everlasting love.
In the Bible, myrtle symbolizes God's promise of peaceful times
(for example, "Instead of briers the myrtle will grow. This will
be for the LORD's renown, for an everlasting sign, which will not
be destroyed" [Isa. 55:13]); and branches of myrtle were used
to decorate during the Feast of Tabernacles ("Go out into the
hill country and bring back branches from olive and wild olive
trees, and from myrtles, palms and shade trees, to make booths"
[Neh. 8:15]).

In the eighteenth century, it was customary for bridesmaids
to plant myrtle in the couple's garden — one plant on each side
of their door. If the plants thrived, superstition had it the bridesmaids would have happy marriages. Another superstition of
this period said that the woman who caught a bride's bouquet
containing myrtle would marry soon — *if* the myrtle bloomed.

Other Flowers

The herb rosemary has been associated with weddings since
ancient times. During Roman weddings, sprigs of rosemary
were a common decoration, thought to bring good luck. The
ancient Greeks considered ivy (which stays green year-round)
a symbol of everlasting love. In early history, brides also carried herbs specifically chosen to ward off evil spirits. In ancient
Greece, Rome, and Egypt, brides carried wheat to ensure fertility. In the Bible, wheat represents God's goodness and is listed
among the things the Lord used to bless his people ("For the

LORD your God is bringing you into a good land ... a land with wheat and barley, vines and fig trees, pomegranates, olive oil and honey" [Deut. 8:7–8]). Roses also were common in early weddings because they were the flower of Venus, the Roman goddess of love.

Strewing Flowers

The custom of strewing petals on the ground dates to biblical times, when the aroma of fresh and dried flowers helped perfume the air. In the Elizabethan era, children dropped rose petals or lavender down the wedding aisle so that the bride might tread upon them, releasing a luxurious scent as she passed by. The very first flower girls were probably seen in pagan weddings, where they carried wheat (a symbol of fertility) down the aisle and carried it to the altar.

The Bridal Bouquet

The ancients carried bouquets of herbs for several reasons. While decoration was surely one of them, most bridal bouquets were also part of pagan fertility rituals. In addition, many bouquets were designed to keep evil spirits at bay. Chives and garlic, being thought most advantageous for this purpose, were commonly found in bridal bouquets.

Christian brides often forwent bouquets and instead held a single handkerchief or a Bible bound in white cloth or leather. Despite the fact that many bridal gowns were trimmed with flowers and most wedding sites were decorated with blooms, it wasn't until the mid-Victorian era that most Christian brides once again began carrying small bouquets.

The Groom's Flowers

The cherished tradition of the groom wearing a small arrangement of flowers on his lapel also dates to ancient times, when grooms wore wreaths atop their heads in hopes of a fertile marriage. By the Elizabethan era, wreaths were exchanged for miniature bouquets, called nosegays; in the Victoria era, boutonnieres (or small arrangements of flowers worn on the lapel) became the norm.

Planting Wedding Flowers

The idea of rooting and planting flowers used in the wedding ceremony was firmly established by Queen Victoria. She planted her bridal flowers in her garden and then used cuttings from the plants for all of her daughters' weddings. It's a delightful tradition, still employed by many today. An ivy plant grown from the bride's bouquet can be a joyfully sentimental item, and a rosebush planted in the couple's yard may, each spring, remind them of their vows.

chapter 30

gifts for the wedding party

the custom of giving gifts to the wedding party probably began in ancient times. Such gifts were a way for families to brag about their wealth (only wealthy families could afford the most impressive gifts) and for brides and grooms to express their genuine thanks. Traditionally, even up into the Victorian era, the gifts came from the groom. As the nineteenth century came to a close, gifts from the bride began to be customary also.

In the Elizabethan era, grooms gave bridesmaids and groomsmen small but luxurious tokens, such as silk handkerchiefs and lace. By the eighteenth century, gloves were a common gift for both sexes. When Queen Victoria wed, she gave each of her bridesmaids a brooch of precious stones. Bits of jewelry were common gifts throughout the Victorian era, as were handkerchiefs and scarves, perfume, and small knickknacks.

chapter 31

groom's attire

before the mid-nineteenth century, grooms wore their best clothes — whether a toga or breeches and a wig. The Bible mentions that the Hebrew groom "decks himself with ornaments" (Isa. 61:10 NKJV); perhaps he was more the center of attention than the bride. It was the Victorians, however, who invented modern masculine wedding attire.

At formal weddings, Victorian grooms wore white tie and tails. Less formal, at-home weddings found the groom wearing a three-piece suit and a frock coat. The Victorians also invented the modern tuxedo, which is the most common wedding attire for men today.

chapter 32

jumping the broom

during the days of slavery, Africans forcibly brought to America to be slaves could not legally wed. Nonetheless, wedding ceremonies were still held among slaves. With their masters' permission, the couple stood among witnesses, sometimes with an older black male to act as minister, and said their vows. Then they literally jumped over a broom.

The tradition of jumping the broom was virtually lost when U.S. slavery ended in the mid-nineteenth century, but the 1976 novel *Roots* brought it back to light. Today, many black Americans incorporate broom jumping into their weddings.

Although some people have tried to argue otherwise, jumping the broom is not an African tradition; however, in some areas of Africa, brooms did symbolize the establishment of new households. Modern writers claim the straws of the broom symbolize the family, and the handle, God.

Interestingly, broom jumping dates back much further than U.S. slavery. In ancient pagan cultures, like those of the Welsh and Scottish, jumping the broom was a popular wedding tradition. At such weddings, newlyweds were told to jump over the broom and "jump from one life into another." In some cases, a pagan priest or priestess would then sweep behind the couple, saying, "May all evil influences be swept out of your life."

chapter 33

kissing at the ceremony's end

Since ancient Roman times, kissing has completed many contracts; this custom gave rise to the saying "Seal it with a kiss." Originally, when the bride and groom kissed at the end of the wedding ceremony, everyone knew this was the completion of their covenant. The kiss was the "seal" that made the deal legally binding. For this reason, there was a time when brides married in the Church of England also kissed the minister.

Later, more romantic ideas about the origin of the kiss were created; one rumor has it that at the kiss, the bride and groom mingle their souls, becoming one.

chapter 34

leaving the ceremony

When the newlyweds leave the church, some sort of leaving tradition has almost always been in place. Perhaps the most familiar of all these is the tossing of rice, which the guests do as the newlyweds leave the wedding site or reception. In ancient times, the Greeks tossed biscuit crumbs over the head of the bride; the idea was that the wheat in the biscuits would magically affect the bride and make her more fertile. The ancient Romans followed suit, breaking cake over the bride's head to make her more "fruitful." Sometimes plain grain was used instead.

We really don't know if early Christians adopted this custom, but it might have made sense, given that the Bible uses wheat to represent God's goodness and blessing (see Deut. 8:7–8, for example). Nobody knows for certain why rice was eventually substituted for grain, but some speculate it was a matter of economics: rice became less costly than wheat. This must have happened before the mid-nineteenth century, because during the Victorian era, when it was considered vulgar to have strangers realize you were a newlywed, one nineteenth-century novel depicts the main characters laying newspaper on the floor of their hotel room and carefully shaking the rice off their clothes, so as not to attract attention.

When the media told us rice might cause illness or death to birds (because in some cases it swells in their stomachs), many brides chose to toss birdseed instead. However, some churches and wedding sites no longer allow birdseed because it prompts wild grasses to grow in their lawns and gardens. (But perhaps the least pleasant part of birdseed tossing is the mess of bird droppings it tends to leave behind.)

In recent years, releasing butterflies has become popular. Most bridal magazines these days contain ads for butterflies that can be purchased already boxed, ready to fly away once the box is opened, creating an excellent photo opportunity. Unfortunately, the actual results can be disappointing, since some butterflies arrive dead or die soon after being released (due to unfriendly climates).

Tossing rose petals over the bride and groom is another popular variation of the old custom. The result is striking and lightly scents the air. This tradition also dates back to ancient times, when roses were widely known as the flower of Venus, the Roman goddess of love. Usually the rose petals are fresh, but some brides like to dry the roses their fiancé gave them and use their petals for the tossing ritual. However, unless your fiancé gives you roses every day (or you're engaged for a long period of time), you may need to supplement the petals he gives you with those from a local florist.

Loose lavender also is sold for the purpose of tossing, and its scent certainly makes it a pleasant choice. Lavender also had great meaning for early Christians. They believed Adam and Eve took lavender out of the garden of Eden, and when baby Jesus' clothes were washed, Mary let them dry on lavender bushes. For these reasons, a cross of lavender was sometimes hung in early Christian homes.

Currently, the most popular leaving tradition is probably blowing bubbles. It's whimsical, beautiful, and fun for the guests. Brides need not worry about getting smacked in the eye with rice (ouch!), but their dress (as well as the dresses of other women) may become water stained.

One leaving tradition that is still approved by almost everybody (because it doesn't cause harm and doesn't leave a mess behind) is the ringing of bells. Many modern brides now supply their guests with small handbells to be chimed joyously as they exit the church. This practice is reminiscent of several passages in the Bible in which the ringing of bells is a reminder of God's holiness (Exod. 28:35; Zech. 14:20).

chapter 35

music

music has always been associated with festivities, including weddings; a biblical wedding feast was not complete without plenty of music and dancing.

Today the wedding music we recognize most is known as "Here Comes the Bride," but it's really Wagner's "Bridal Chorus" from the opera *Lohengrin*. Some churches forbid the use of this music on the grounds that it comes from a pagan story.

Perhaps the second best-known wedding music is Mendelssohn's "Wedding March" from *A Midsummer Night's Dream*. This opera also rests heavily on pagan myths and legends, and some churches have banned its use in weddings. In addition, neither *Lohengrin* or *Midsummer* depict very healthy marriages.

For these reasons, many modern couples choose other pieces of music. If you still want something traditional, Pachelbel's "Canon in D" is beautiful and ideal for walking up the aisle. "Trumpet Voluntary" by Purcell is also a good choice, as is "Postlude in G Minor" by Handel. Charpentier's "Processional" from *Te Deum* is time-honored, as is Beethoven's "Midnight Blue." For the recessional, "Ode to Joy" by Beethoven is a classic choice, as is Vivaldi's "Autumn" from *The Four Seasons*.

If you want a dash of something slightly more modern but still classic, the "Wedding Processional" from *The Sound of Music* and the famous Louis Armstrong tune "What a Wonderful World" are popular choices. Other modern songs that are good choices for the ceremony include "Unforgettable" (famously sung by Nat King Cole), "Can't Help Falling in Love with You" (Elvis Presley), "Masterpiece" (Atlantic Star), "The Best Is Yet to Come" (Nancy Wilson), and "In My Life" (the Beatles). Anything that sets a romantic or reverent tone (and is easy to walk down the aisle to) is appropriate.

For songs with Christian meaning, you might consider "I Have Not Love" (based on 1 Corinthians 13), "Household of Faith" (popularly sung by Steve Green), "The Commitment Song" (Gary Barlow), "Cherish the Treasure," "This is the Day," and "Only God Could Love You More."

At the reception, almost any type of music is appropriate. If you want dancing at your wedding, anything with a beat — especially if it's of a romantic nature — works best.

chapter 36

processionals

the practice of walking in a processional to the place of the wedding ceremony dates to biblical times. The bride and groom each traveled with a party of family and friends who were assigned the duty of "protecting" them. No doubt part of the reason for this tradition was to ensure that no cold feet sent the bride or groom running. By the medieval era, it was common for brides and grooms to walk to the church together, their friends and family in a merry party alongside them, singing and tossing flowers. Hebrew brides arrived at the wedding site under canopies; in the eighteenth century, European brides sometimes arrived on horseback; in Germany, white carriages were favored.

The order of wedding processionals has varied over the centuries and probably wasn't solidified until the late eighteenth or early nineteenth century. In today's traditional Jewish ceremony, the rabbi enters first, followed by the grandparents of the bride and groom. Next, the groomsmen enter and stand under the *huppah*, or wedding canopy. Then the best man enters, followed by the groom, who is escorted by both of his parents. Next, the bridesmaids and honor attendant enter. Finally, the bride enters, accompanied by both her parents.

Christian processionals are based on this form but vary slightly. In Roman Catholic churches, the priest may greet the bride and groom at the entrance of the church and lead them to the altar. In other churches, the priest, groom, and best man wait at the altar. The groomsmen follow, then the bridesmaids, ring bearer, flower girl, and honor attendants. Finally, the bride enters, walking to the left of her father.

In Protestant churches, the pastor, groom, and best man generally enter from a front or side door as the music begins (or just before the music begins); then they wait at the altar. From the back of the church, the groomsmen and bridesmaids enter (sometimes together, sometimes with the women following the men), then the ring bearer, flower girl, and honor attendants. When the bride enters, walking to the left of her father, the guests stand. The father may remain at the altar for the beginning of the ceremony, or he may be seated and later rise when the minister asks who is giving the bride away.

chapter 37

standing on the left

no one knows for certain why the bride stands to the left of the groom during the wedding ceremony, but some believe this arrangement dates to a time when brides were stolen, and the groom wanted his right hand free in case he needed to grab his sword and ward off the bride's angry family.

In traditional Jewish ceremonies, however, the bride and her family stand on the right, and the groom and his family stand on the left. In addition, during military weddings, the bride stands to the groom's right in order to avoid brushing up against his sword.

chapter 38

taking the husband's last name

Since time immemorial, brides have adopted their husbands' surnames. No doubt this tradition began as a part of "the two becoming one." Even so, throughout history, the practice of using both the bride's maiden name and her husband's last name has gone in and out of fashion. Although the hyphenated last name is thought of as a modern invention, eighteenth- and nineteenth-century brides (and their children) sometimes kept both names — the bride's maiden name becoming a sort of middle name. However, it wasn't until twentieth-century feminism came along that the idea of not using the husband's surname emerged.

Nothing is inherently wrong with any of the above practices, but whatever choice is made, both the bride and the groom should be comfortable with the decision. Some men still feel wounded if their wives opt not to take their last names, so an open conversation about the topic is a good idea.

unity candles

Perhaps no other wedding tradition stirs up as much controversy as the unity candle. Actually, the unity "candle" is *three* candles: one large one representing the couple and two smaller candles — one representing the bride's family and the other representing the groom's family. Another popular variation on unity candle symbolism is that the smaller candles represent the bride and groom, and the larger candle, their marriage. In an old Christian tradition called the "candlelight blessing," the flame of the candle is a symbol of Christ, the Light of the World. With that in mind, a growing number of brides and grooms prefer to think of the larger unity candle as symbolic of Christ, while the two smaller ones represent the couple.

But in all cases, the unity candle is a symbol of — you guessed it — unity. The tradition is only thirty or forty years old, but when you start probing its history, controversy waltzes in. A common rumor is that unity candles originated on a soap opera. Some brides have told me their priest or pastor advised them to skip unity candles altogether, given this history. However, evidence to back up this theory is hard to come by, and it's unlikely that a soap opera would invent — from scratch — a wedding tradition. On the other hand, it's certainly possible that a soap opera *popularized* the custom and that after seeing a unity candle ceremony on television, many brides wished to incorporate a similar one in their own weddings. But popularizing a custom is quite a different thing from inventing it.

Another oft-heard rumor is that unity candles originated in the Roman Catholic Church. However, most Roman Catholic churches don't even permit unity candle ceremonies. According to Roman Catholic officiates, unity candles are redundant because vows, rings, and communion are all symbols of unity. So why, they ask, add a new custom to the older, more sacred ones? In addition, the United States Conference of Catholic Bishops feels the symbolism of the unity candle is seriously incorrect. When the smaller candles are extinguished after the larger candle is lit, they say it symbolizes that the bride and groom's old lives are over. Most ministers and Christian marriage counselors would agree that the bride and groom's old lives don't die; instead, their lives *blend* with each other. Still, this problem is solved in many Protestant ceremonies by not extinguishing the smaller candles.

Nonetheless, the actual origin of the unity candle is obscure; it isn't firmly traceable to formal wedding customs anywhere in the world. Interestingly, Eastern European Slavic countries claim to be the originators of the unity candle tradition — but there's no real evidence to back up this claim. At the other end of the spectrum, at least one Presbyterian minister has announced on the Internet that after the Marriage Rite was revised and shortened, unity candles were invented to lengthen the ceremony for the purpose of photographic opportunity. This explanation hardly seems likely, however. And so we're left wondering about the true origin of the unity candle.

The unity candle remains a popular tradition despite the fact that some churches don't allow open flames in the sanctuary for safety reasons. (Couples typically work around this restriction by lighting their unity candle at the reception.) The custom has even begun to extend beyond the wedding day, with some couples relighting the candles on their anniversaries.

Couples having outdoor ceremonies often approach the unity candle tradition with trepidation. At my own wedding, which was held outdoors on what turned out to be a windy day, we attempted the lighting and succeeded for only a moment before the flames were blown out by the wind. Those who are superstitious might see this as a bad omen, but it didn't bother my husband or me in the least. One clever couple I know planned for potential wind by using hurricane lamps in their outdoor wedding. Another couple, who had a beach wedding, used large, Hawaiian-style party torches in place of candles.

Typically the unity candle ritual begins after the couple is pronounced husband and wife. Here's how it works: The two smaller candles are lit just before the wedding ceremony and remain lit throughout. Sometimes the parents of the bride and groom light the candles. Occasionally the smaller candles are lit after the bride and groom begin the unity candle ritual; typically this is when the mothers (or some other family members) are being included in the custom. The candles are typically arranged with the large candle between the smaller ones.

When the couple is ready to commence with the unity candle, they move to wherever the candles have been sitting. Preferably the candles are set up in such a way that the guests can easily see the unity candle ceremony. (If possible, the couple should face the guests instead of putting their backs to them.)

The bride and groom each pick up a lighted candle. If a family member has pre-lit them, the groom picks up the candle from his side of the family, and the bride uses the one from her side of the family. Simultaneously the bride and groom use their small candles to light the large candle. For Christian couples, the lighting is a lovely way to symbolize their union — and the Light that unites them as one.

chapter 40

VOWS

♦

I n the Bible, the earliest mention of vows appears in Genesis, when Jacob promises he will take the Lord as his God. During Old Testament times, vows were used in a wide variety of situations and culminated in a covenant.

The Bible refers to marriage as a covenant (for example, see Malachi 2:14: "The LORD is acting as the witness between you and the wife of your youth, ... the wife of your marriage covenant"), and since covenants (by their nature) involve taking vows, both Hebrews and early Christians said wedding vows. Modern brides and grooms make their vows to each other, certainly — but their vows, like Jacob's vow, are also promises to the Lord.

We don't have a record of wedding vows during biblical times, and we don't know when vows as we now know them began. Today, it's not uncommon for couples to at least consider writing their own wedding vows. Many associate this "new tradition" with the 1960s and '70s; however, it's not unreasonable to assume that the first wedding vows were much like Jacob's vow to God — not out of a book but straight from the heart and relatively unplanned (see Gen. 28:20). Historians know with certainty that custom vows were common among pagan brides and grooms. The groom typically asked something as simple as "Will you marry me?" and the bride answered back, "You betcha."

It was only in churches and synagogues that standardized vows were firmly established. Over the years, they've changed some, but not much. For example, traditional Jewish vows may sound familiar:

RABBI: Do you, John, take Jane to be your wife?

MAN: I do.

RABBI: Do you promise to love, cherish, and protect her, whether in good fortune or in adversity, and to seek with her a life hallowed by the faith of Israel?

MAN: I do.

RABBI: Do you, Jane, take John to be your husband?

WOMAN: I do.

RABBI: Do you promise to love, cherish, and protect him, whether in good fortune or in adversity, and to seek with him a life hallowed by the faith of Israel?

WOMAN: I do.

RABBI: John, as you place this ring upon the finger of Jane, speak to her these vows: "With this ring be thou consecrated unto me as my wife, according to the law of God, and the faith of Israel." Jane, as you place this ring upon the finger of John, speak to him these vows: "With this ring, be thou consecrated unto me, as my husband, according to the law of God, and the faith of Israel."

The *Book of Common Prayer* (published in 1662) puts the Christian vows in these words:

MINISTER: Wilt thou have this Woman to be thy wedded wife, to live together after God's ordinance in the holy estate of Matrimony? Wilt thou love her, comfort her, honour, and keep her in sickness and in health; and, forsaking all others, keep thee only unto her, so long as ye both shall live?

MAN: I will.

MINISTER: Wilt thou have this Man to be thy wedded husband, to live together after God's ordinance in the holy estate of Matrimony? Wilt thou love him, comfort him, honour, and keep him in sickness and in health; and, forsaking all others, keep thee only unto him, so long as ye both shall live?

WOMAN: I will.

MAN: I, John, take thee, Jane, to be my wedded Wife, to have and to hold from this day forward, for better for worse, for richer for poorer, in sickness and in health, to love and to cherish, till death us do part, according to God's holy ordinance; and thereto I give thee my troth.

WOMAN: I, Jane, take thee, John, to be my wedded Husband, to have and to hold from this day forward, for better for worse, for richer for poorer, in sickness and in health, to love and to cherish, till death us do part, according to God's holy ordinance; and thereto I give thee my troth.

Usually with a little revising of "wilts" and "thous," modern Christian churches use the very same vows.

If the Judeo-Christian history behind vows doesn't inspire you, then you might also consider this: your guests may benefit most from what we've come to know as traditional vows. "Yes, vows are 99 percent about the bride and groom," one married woman told me recently, "but in some way, the vows are for the married guests too. When I sit at a wedding, I can't help but hold my husband's hand, recalling our own wedding day, how much I love him, and how important our vows are."

If you still think you want to write your own vows, the first thing you might consider is *why* you want to have vows that are different from traditional wedding vows. As one bride told me, "We sat down, determined to write our own vows. We made a list of just what it was we were agreeing to by getting married. We talked about how we'd stay faithful to each other no matter what, how we'd be together forever — not just until we didn't feel 'in love' anymore. We talked about how we were a team.... But when we wrote a draft of our vows, we realized that everything we wanted to say to each other, and to our families and friends, and to God, was already there in the wedding vows everyone knows today. And it was said in a much more clear and meaningful way!"

chapter 41

wedding bells

Once upon a time, the sound of bells chiming was thought to keep away evil spirits. The ringing of bells was also said to keep couples from arguing and remind them of their wedding vows. For these reasons, a traditional Irish wedding gift is a bell. These bits of lore may also be the reason behind the wedding reception tradition of ringing handbells in order to "make" the bride and groom kiss.

However, the use of bells for weddings goes back even further in time. In the Bible, bells are associated with holiness. Ancient Hebrew high priests wore bells on their robes (Exod. 28:35: "The sound of the bells will be heard when he enters the Holy Place before the LORD and when he comes out, so that he will not die"). These bells alerted everyone that they were coming before God. This may be one reason Christian churches originally began using tower bells to call the congregation to worship. Today the use of bells at weddings harkens back to a time when the soft jingle of a priest's robe prepared everyone for the presence of God.

chapter 42

wedding rings

Wedding rings date at least as far back as the ancient Egyptians. In fact, the whole idea behind wedding bands may be connected to the fact that the Egyptian symbol for eternity is a circle. However, we also know that in Old Testament times, Hebrew men used rings as a seal — part of their signature on contracts. Indeed, Hebrew weddings were not considered complete until the groom gave the bride some physical object; a gift worth at least a penny was required to complete the covenant. This contractual significance may also explain why rings were originally used in weddings.

The very earliest wedding bands were fashioned from leather, bone, ivory, and sometimes even grass. Later, iron, gold, silver, and other metals were substituted.

But the wedding band hasn't always been worn on the left hand's fourth finger. For example, until the eighteenth century, Roman Catholics wore their wedding rings on the right hand, and Greek Orthodox brides wore their rings on the left hand before the ceremony, then moved them to the right hand after marriage. Some brides continue to follow these customs today. In addition, some Scandinavian women follow the old practice of wearing a ring apiece for engagement, marriage, and motherhood. King Edward VI designated the *third* finger of the left hand as the "official" wedding ring finger; the 1549 *Book of Common Prayer* also declared this the "proper" finger.

So why do most people of the modern world wear their wedding bands on the left hand, fourth finger? A practical reason for wearing the ring on the left hand is that most people are right-handed; therefore, wearing the wedding band on the left hand means it is less likely to get damaged. As for the fourth finger, we know the ancient Egyptians placed their wedding rings here; scholars suggest this was because they believed there was a vein that ran from that finger all the way up to the heart.

By medieval times, the placement of the ring had taken on clear Christian meaning. During the ceremony, the groom held the ring over the bride's hand. Beginning with the left thumb, he said, "In the name of the Father, in the name of the Son, and in the name of the Holy Ghost," and with each name, moved the ring over one finger. When he said, "Amen," he placed the ring on what is known today as the "ring finger."

Incidentally, there are those who say the wedding band symbolizes servitude — because, the theory goes, all brides are supposed to be under the dominion of their husbands, and the ring is a sign that they are "owned." However, men also wear wedding bands (and have for a long time; the 1546 *English Prayer Book* stipulates this arrangement), so if the ring represents servitude, it clearly symbolizes the fact that husband and wife serve *each other*.

part 3

post-ceremony traditions

chapter 43

anniversaries

tradition is strongly associated with three wedding anniversaries: the first anniversary, the "silver anniversary," and the "gold anniversary."

A couple's first wedding anniversary is traditionally marked by eating the top layer of their wedding cake. Back when these were heavy fruitcakes that could be stored for a long period of time, couples reserved a portion by wrapping it in a piece of paper and putting it in the pantry or icebox. On the night of their first anniversary, they ate the cake for dessert. When wedding cakes became modern white, fluffy affairs, brides started storing the top layer in the freezer. Today this tradition is becoming less and less common; cake just doesn't taste that great after sitting in the freezer for a year. However, in an attempt to keep the tradition alive, some bakers are now offering a "free anniversary cake" when couples purchase their wedding cake.

Although it's fairly uncommon today, in the past, when a couple's twenty-fifth anniversary rolled around, a large celebration was organized. Engraved invitations were distributed, and a lavish dinner with dancing was usually held. Since twenty-fifth anniversaries are called "silver anniversaries," guests usually brought gifts of silver. Often the celebration began the same moment the marriage ceremony took place, and whenever possible, the bridesmaids and groomsmen were present. A wedding cake, at least as extravagant as the original, was typically included, and small silver favors were given to the guests.

An alternative (but still traditional) way of celebrating a silver anniversary was for the couple to send gifts of silver to other couples who had recently celebrated or were soon going to celebrate their own twenty-fifth anniversary.

For couples married for fifty years, another large celebration used to be common. Again, engraved cards were sent out, and the bridesmaids and groomsmen were ideally in attendance. The dinner for this "golden anniversary" was elaborate and included a grand cake. The wife was encouraged to wear something from her wedding day and often carried a bridal-like bouquet. Presents of gold were considered appropriate, and sometimes gold charms were included as favors for the guests.

No one is sure why certain wedding anniversaries are associated with particular types of gifts. However, we do know the tradition of silver and gold anniversaries dates at least to medieval times, when German husbands gave their wives a silver garland for their twenty-fifth anniversary and a gold wreath for their fiftieth anniversary. Other anniversary associations may be old, but they weren't in widespread use until the American National Retail Jeweler Association formalized a list in 1937. Today alternative lists exist, but that early list is still most traditional:

1st Paper	7th Copper	13th Lace	35th Coral or Jade
2nd Cotton	8th Bronze	14th Ivory	40th Ruby
3rd Leather	9th Pottery	15th Crystal	45th Sapphire
4th Flowers	10th Tin	20th China	50th Gold
5th Wood	11th Steel	25th Silver	55th Emerald
6th Iron	12th Silk	30th Pearl	60th Diamond

chapter 44

bedding

beginning in ancient times, it was customary to "bed" the newlywed couple. Ancient Romans sent the bride into the couple's bedroom, accompanied by what was probably the original matron of honor: an older, happily married woman. The matron helped the bride into her nightclothes and tucked her into bed. Then the groomsmen brought in the groom, undressed him, and helped him into bed.

This tradition lasted well into the seventeenth century in Europe, growing progressively less tasteful as time went on. Larger groups of people began entering the bedroom and "helping" the bride and groom; in fact, it's believed the custom of tossing the garter originated with undressing the bride during bedding. In some cultures and eras, witnesses were left in the bedroom so that everyone would know for certain that the marriage was consummated.

Ancient Jewish custom was more modest. After the wedding ceremony, as guests made their way to the reception, the couple was led to a private room for *yichud*, or "the unity." Here they broke the fast that began that morning. Consummation of the marriage also sometimes took place. No one is really certain if this tradition was practiced during biblical times; some scholars think the Bible is speaking of *yichud* when it mentions a canopy or tent in Psalm 19:4–5 ("In the heavens he has pitched a tent for the sun, which is like a bridegroom coming forth from his pavilion") and Joel 2:16 ("Let the bridegroom leave his room and the bride her chamber").

Today Jewish couples sometimes still practice *yichud* — not to consummate their marriage but to spend ten or fifteen minutes alone before the hustle and bustle of the reception. Some Christian couples also are now adopting this "breathing time" into their wedding rituals.

cakes

The first wedding cakes probably date to the ancient Greeks and Romans. However, these weren't the light, spongy, white-frosted affairs we know today. Rather, the ancients offered wheat loaves or biscuits to their wedding guests, who in turn sprinkled broken pieces over the heads of the couple to wish them fertility. The Romans also offered these wedding cakes to Jupiter, their "supreme god."

We don't know if the ancient Hebrews had wedding cakes, but it's possible. During biblical times, Hebrews often ate sweet cakes at celebrations. These were filled with honey, which throughout the Bible symbolizes God's goodness (see Exod. 3:8, for example).

Some historians also believe wedding cakes were likely used by early Christians, as the "breaking of bread" (begun by Jesus during the Lord's Supper; see Matt. 26:26) has always been an important custom in the Christian community.

In the Middle Ages, wedding guests baked their own small biscuit-like cakes and brought them to the ceremony, potluck style. Leftovers were given to the needy, and guests were offered a piece to take home. Around this same time, it also became customary to stack these small cakes into a pile; guests attempted to make the pile as tall as possible, thinking it might help ensure prosperity for the couple. The couple kissed over the mound, and if it didn't tumble to the ground, they were supposed to be blessed with many children.

Legend has it that a French baker, who was visiting England in the 1660s, hated the thought of all those little cakes falling over (as they were apt to do), making a mess and wasting food. So he created the first multilayered cake using larger cakes and white sugar frosting.

By the seventeenth century, baking methods had improved, and dry biscuit-like cakes were replaced with moist, rich fruitcakes. The wealthy topped these with white sugar frosting. (White sugar was expensive, and its use on wedding cakes was considered lavish.)

For those who weren't wealthy, a "bride's pie" was sometimes served instead of a cake. This was mincemeat, sweetbread, or mutton pie — sometimes with a ring baked inside. The first unmarried guest to find the ring was supposed to marry soon.

It wasn't until the nineteenth century, however, when baking powder, baking soda, and finer flours were beginning to be used, that something like the modern wedding cake began to appear. Piping tubes were invented in the 1840s, enabling more lavish cake decoration, and the new wedding cakes were light, white, and fluffy. Queen Victoria and Prince Albert had such a cake at their 1840 wedding. It was a monster, weighing some three hundred pounds and measuring nine feet in diameter. (According to *The Guinness Book of World Records*, the world's largest wedding cake weighed 15,032 pounds and was made for a 2004 bridal show.)

Making cakes was difficult and time-consuming in the Victorian era, but cakes, as opposed to pies or biscuits, soon became a "necessity" at every wedding, no matter how poor the bride and groom. Victorian cookbooks nearly always contained information on baking wedding cakes, the recipes often taking up several pages. Amateur bakers had to test the flour for lightness, remove a few straws from a broom (to test the cake's doneness), clean and clear the entire kitchen, make certain the windows were open so the room wouldn't get too hot, clear the stove of ashes, and beat the ingredients by hand. It was a real pain, and the letters and diaries of American women are filled with tales of trying to make wedding cakes under less than ideal circumstances.

Stacked cakes were not the norm until the 1850s. These tricky-to-make concoctions were prepared by professional bakers — which meant only the wealthy could afford them. The first stacked wedding cakes are said to have been inspired by the spire of St. Bride's Church in London, whose tower resembles stacked hatboxes. The first notable use of a stacked cake was at the 1858 wedding of Queen Victoria's eldest daughter, Princess Victoria. This cake was even grander than the Queen's own wedding cake, measuring at least six feet high — although only the bottom layer was edible.

Harkening back to the Middle Ages, when wedding guests were given small cakes to take home, the "groom's cake" began appearing in the nineteenth century. The groom's cake was offered in addition to the wedding cake and was of the old style: heavy, dark, and fruit-filled. It was usually passed out to guests as they started toward home. Today when groom's cakes are seen, they're often chocolate and are sometimes served at the rehearsal dinner instead of the reception. Superstition has it that if an unmarried woman places a piece of groom's cake under her pillow, she'll dream of the man she's going to marry.

The ancient Romans probably started the custom of the bride and groom eating a piece of cake together, but many cultures practiced variations on this. Jewish couples drank from the same glass of wine, German couples ate from the same bowl of soup, and Chinese couples shared honey. When the newly-weds eat a piece of cake together, they are symbolizing two becoming one. The joint cutting of the wedding cake (which didn't become customary until the early part of the twentieth century) represents the first task the husband and wife share in their life together.

chapter 46

carrying the bride over the threshold

the custom of the groom carrying the bride over the threshold of their new home dates to ancient times. Roman brides were led around the couple's hearth — a vital part of every home and the place where pagan sacrifices were made. Superstition had it that if the bride tripped or fell on her way to the hearth, the marriage would be plagued; therefore, the bride was carried into the house and safely deposited in front of the hearth.

In later times, it was considered important for the groom to step carefully over the threshold; in many parts of Europe, evil spirits were thought to linger in the ground, and witchcraft suggested that doorways were magic portals. Today in India, for fear of evil spirits, the groom is often carried over the threshold first; then he lifts the bride to safety.

dancing

dancing has been part of wedding celebrations since biblical times. Ancient Hebrew weddings included music and dancing both before and after the ceremony. Generally, women danced together in a group, but when both sexes danced, they danced separately — men in one group, women in another. For the Hebrews, dancing was a way of worshiping God and expressing joy. (Consider, for example, Jeremiah 31:4: "I will build you up again and you will be rebuilt, O Virgin Israel. Again you will take up your tambourines and go out to dance with the joyful.")

Dancing continued to be an important part of wedding celebrations throughout the early Christian era and into the first part of the nineteenth century. During the Victorian era, however, dancing suddenly became taboo at the weddings of the middle and upper class. Evening weddings occasionally included formal dancing, for which the bride was first paired with the best man and the groom with the maid of honor, but dancing was generally considered inappropriate at receptions. This all changed in the 1920s, when dancing at weddings came back with a vengeance.

The dollar dance, or money dance, is a custom that is still in widespread practice today. It was probably introduced to the United States during the late nineteenth century, brought here by immigrants from European countries. In some instances, men and women line up and wait for the opportunity to dance with the bride or groom; each dance costs one dollar. In a more common variation, male guests may dance with the bride only if they give her a dollar bill or pin the money onto her dress.

In the Ukraine, the father of the bride usually begins the money dance (and perhaps this tradition gave rise to the twentieth-century custom of the bride enjoying a special dance with her father). Hungarian tradition has the bride remove her shoes and put them in the middle of the dance floor as a receptacle for the money. In Yugoslavia, the money is handed to the best man for safekeeping. In Italy, the bride carries a purse to put the money in.

Originally, money dances were designed to help the couple get off to a good start financially, but today some people find the custom distasteful. A modern variation is to have guests write well wishes on slips of paper and hand them to or pin them on the bride.

chapter 48

favors

the first wedding favors — small tokens given to the wedding guests by the newlyweds — were the biscuits seen at ancient Greek and Roman weddings. Although we don't have a record of Hebrews and early Christians passing out wedding favors, it's likely they gave flowers, nuts, and dried fruit, just as other ancient cultures did.

By the Elizabethan era, ribbon bows (given to and worn by both men and women) were a common favor — a tradition that lasted well into the early twentieth century. The wealthy sometimes gave favors of jewelry, handmade gloves, hand-painted fans, and other extravagant items.

Beginning in the mid-twentieth century, commercial items such as printed matchbooks and napkins came into fashion; but today the old standbys of nuts and candy tend to be most popular.

chapter 49

honeymoons

many theories exist about the origin of the honeymoon. The most common explanation is that honeymoons began in an era when some brides were captured and stolen. The groom, it's said, had to keep the bride tucked away somewhere until her family was no longer angry. These early honeymoons lasted about a month — just enough time for tempers to cool. Since ancient people usually marked the months by the phases of the moon, the "moon" in honeymoon may refer to this month-long period of hiding.

Yet the tradition of honeymoons goes all the way back to the days of Moses. In Deuteronomy 24:5, God implements a law forbidding grooms to work during the first year of their marriage. For a whole year, the bridegroom was to stay home "and bring happiness to the wife he has married."

Although the Bible does not refer to this one-year period specifically as a "honeymoon," it's not entirely unthinkable that the term may have sprung from the Bible. Throughout the Scriptures, honey is used to describe goodness. (For example, see Exodus 3:8, where the Lord describes Israel as "a land flowing with milk and honey," and Song of Songs 4:11, where the groom describes his bride's mouth as being as sweet as honey.)

A more probable explanation for the term *honeymoon* comes from ancient German customs. For the first month after the wedding, Germanic newlyweds drank from a cup of mead (honey wine). Some historians say this period was called "the month of honey" or "the moon of honey" and that over time, this phrase was simplified to "honeymoon."

While ancient Hebrews may have had year-long honeymoons, throughout history many honeymoons were much shorter. A month-long honeymoon wasn't uncommon for those of means; in fact, this tradition was fairly common well into the twentieth century. For those with little wealth, honeymoons were often nonexistent. For everyone else, honeymoons usually lasted a few weeks; today most honeymoons last a week or two.

chapter 50

receiving line

◆

In biblical times, guests crowded the bride and groom to offer their congratulations after the wedding. Historians believe it wasn't until the eighteenth century that wealthier families started to bring some order to this custom, introducing the receiving line.

For less formal receptions held in modest homes, antique etiquette books suggest that the bride and groom stand under a bell. This made it easier for guests to find the couple and offer their congratulations to the groom and good wishes to the bride. (Traditionally, it's improper to congratulate the bride — presumably because the groom is the one making "the big catch.")

chapter 51

receptions

◆

I n the Bible, long and joyful wedding festivities were held, complete with music, dancing, and wine. Most receptions lasted a week or more and included the whole community. When Samson gave his attendants a riddle to solve, he gave them the full week of wedding festivities to try to come up with the right answer ("If you can give me the answer within the seven days of the feast, I will give you thirty linen garments and thirty sets of clothes" [Judg. 14:12]); and when Jacob married his first wife, his father-in-law also mentioned a week-long reception ("Finish out this daughter's bridal week; then we will give you the younger one also, in return for another seven years of work" [Gen. 29:27]).

Guests dropped everything to attend the festivities and were treated to plenty of food and drink from the bride's family. If either food or wine ran out, the shortage was considered shameful and a serious insult to guests. Therefore, when Christ performed his first miracle, it was an act of compassion for the bride's family (see John 2). The jars Jesus used for this miracle held about twenty to thirty gallons apiece; he created six jars of wine, giving guests at least 120 gallons to drink. Instead of being shamed, the bride's family was honored when the groom sipped Jesus' wine and said to his in-laws: "Everyone brings out the choice wine first and then the cheaper wine after the guests have had too much to drink; but you have saved the best till now" (John 2:10).

Music was also important to biblical wedding celebrations, with musicians playing bells, cymbals, castanets, harps, lutes, flutes, trumpets, and other instruments while guests danced.

It wasn't until the Middle Ages that receptions were generally shortened to one day and became slightly more reserved affairs. However, to this day, feasting and music are important at most wedding receptions.

chapter 52

shoes

the custom of tying shoes to the couple's honeymoon vehicle may have some biblical significance. In Old Testament times, one way to seal a contract was to remove a shoe. For example, Boaz removed his sandal when he promised to marry Ruth. The Bible explains: "Now in earlier times in Israel, for the redemption and transfer of property to become final, one party took off his sandal and gave it to the other. This was the method of legalizing transactions in Israel" (Ruth 4:7).

In the Middle Ages, it was common for European fathers to remove their daughter's left shoe and give it to her groom on the wedding day. In some cases, the shoe was later placed at the head of the marriage bed — a sign of the contract entered into through the wedding ceremony. In Wales, the bride and groom were sometimes given a pair of shoes that were held together with a chain carved from a single piece of wood. This again was a symbol of their marriage covenant.

Tying shoes to the bumper of the couple's "get-away vehicle" may in part be a reminder of the covenant the couple just entered. It may also be connected to an old custom of throwing shoes at people who are beginning a journey. During Tudor times, instead of throwing rice or grain at the newlyweds, wedding guests sometimes threw old shoes at their carriage to wish them a good journey. Even into the 1920s, wedding guests occasionally threw satin slippers at the bride and groom as they left the church.

Sometimes tin cans are tied onto the bumper along with old shoes. These noisemakers were originally meant to scare evil spirits and deter them from following the couple.

toasts

Since at least the Middle Ages, it's been traditional to toast any ladies present at a feast. While this custom has slowly faded, the toasting of the bride has remained common at wedding receptions. However, until the twentieth century, the father of the bride gave the toast, not the best man. Today the bride *and* groom are usually toasted.

(Incidentally, legend has it that the term *toast* dates back to sixteenth-century France, when a small piece of bread was placed at the bottom of wine glasses to prevent any sediment at the bottom of the glass from being drunk.)

Traditionally, toasts are given with the right hand. This indicates friendship, since most people are right-handed and would hold their sword in their right hand. The clinking of glasses also is customary and probably dates to a time when noises were thought to scare off evil spirits.

A traditional Christian toast goes like this:

May God be with you and bless you.
May you see your children's children.
May you be poor in misfortune and rich in blessings.
May you know nothing but happiness from this day forward.

We also know that wine (and perhaps with it, toasting) has been part of wedding festivities since biblical times. Jesus' first miracle was performed when a wedding feast was almost halted because the wine had run out (John 2:1–11).

chapter 54

tossing the garter and bouquet

ncient Roman brides, after being carried over the threshold to the family hearth, lit a torch, blew it out, and tossed it to the wedding guests, who all tried to catch it. Undoubtedly this ritual is the forerunner of both the garter and bouquet toss.

In the fourteenth century, when bedding the bride was a popular custom, the unmarried men taking part in the tradition tried to snatch the bride's garter for good luck. It's believed that brides, not enjoying this manhandling, began removing their garters and flinging them at the crowd, resulting in the tradition of the garter toss. Some historians also believe that during these bedding ceremonies, unmarried women started stealing the bride's stockings in hopes of having some of the bride's good luck rub off on them. Once again, it's believed the bride preferred to remove her own clothing and started throwing her stockings at the crowd. Later, when bedding became socially unacceptable, brides tossed their bouquets to the crowd instead.

In a fifteenth-century custom, the couple's stockings were stolen. Once the couple was tucked in for the night, unmarried guests sat at the foot of the bed, their backs facing the newlyweds. They flung the stockings over their heads, and if they hit the newlyweds, they were supposed to wed soon.

A variation comes from Russia, where the newlyweds ceremoniously removed each other's stockings before retiring on their wedding night; today many Russians throw stockings instead of garters at wedding receptions.

In the Victorian era, some brides carried a bouquet composed of many small bouquets tied together; when it came time to toss, they separated the small bouquets so the ladies present didn't need to fight over a single bunch of flowers. In the twentieth century, brides who wished to preserve their bridal bouquet began using copy bouquets for the toss.

wedding gifts

Until recent times, wedding presents were sent long before the day of the ceremony; etiquette books up through the mid-twentieth century suggested sending the gifts at least two months before the wedding.

What was considered an appropriate gift? Generally, the prettiest and most useful thing one could afford to give. China, silver, glassware, linens, and books were all considered good gifts, and if the giver was close to the bride or groom, money gifts also were suitable. Today all manner of household goods are still fitting wedding gifts, but most presents are given at the reception — not months before the wedding. In recent times, boxes or paper wishing wells have become common at wedding receptions, allowing guests who brought cards, but not presents, to safely deposit them. Gifts of money also may be slipped inside.

However, wedding gifts haven't always been considered appropriate. We don't know for certain when guests began bringing gifts for the bride and groom, but it's not unreasonable to believe this custom dates to biblical times. Hebrew couples usually wore flower crowns on their wedding day and were called "king" and "queen" throughout the celebration. Not only did guests traditionally bring gifts when visiting royalty (see, for example, 1 Samuel 10:27, which notes that some Israelites despised the newly crowned King Saul and "brought him no gifts"), but the groom's friends are known to have offered presents during the betrothal ceremony — so why not at the wedding itself?

Traditionally, anything that guests could afford was welcomed. Often handmade goods or small tokens of sentiment were given, along with practical goods to help furnish the couple's home. The giving of food for the honeymoon also was common. By the nineteenth century, however, many people felt a great deal of pressure to give expensive presents. Wedding presents were frequently displayed during the reception, and guests paraded by, giving little oohs and aahs over the most lavish presents. Given these pressures, late Victorian etiquette books often insisted that the tradition of wedding gifts be abolished. Some nineteenth-century wedding invitations even included the line "No Presents Received."

Nineteenth- and early twentieth-century etiquette books also stressed that fancy china and silver weren't appropriate for every couple. As *The Etiquette of Engagement and Marriage* noted, "Good silver is always a joy, except perhaps when you have to keep it clean. The young wife with only one servant will have to rub up her own silver." Therefore, authors stressed that the situation of every couple should be taken into consideration when giving gifts. Not bad advice, even today.

epilogue

traditions enrich our lives. They help us share deeply spiritual events with others. They allow us to bond with complete strangers and dear loved ones. They help us feel connected to our ancestors. They may even help us testify to our faith in the Lord.

And while it may be difficult to replace classic traditions entirely, there are always new traditions waiting to become classics. If they hold special meaning for you and your groom, there's no reason not to create them. One Christian bride I spoke with while writing this book added biblical foot washing to her wedding ceremony. Other Christian couples have told me they donated their wedding flowers to a local hospital. Another bride mentioned that she and her groom had two wedding cakes made — one for the reception and one for a local shelter. The possibilities for new and meaningful traditions are endless — and may inspire not only your guests but your children and grandchildren for years to come.

Whatever classic or new traditions you include in your wedding, I hope that they will encourage your light to shine. May your marriage be enriched and blessed by the traditions you keep and the Lord you worship.

selected bibliography

Anonymous. *The Habits of Good Society*. New York: Carleton, 1864.

_____. *The Manners That Win*. Minneapolis: Buckeye, 1883.

_____. *Practical Housekeeping*. Minneapolis: Buckeye, 1884.

Chesterfield. *Chesterfield's Art of Letter-Writing and Complete Rules of Etiquette*. New York: Dick & Fitzgerald, 1887.

Devereux, G. R. M. *The Etiquette of Engagement & Marriage*. London: C. Arthur Pearson, 1903.

Diamant, Anita. *The New Jewish Wedding*. New York: Summit Books, 1985.

Eichler, Lillian. *Book of Etiquette*. Oyster Bay, N.Y.: Nelson Doubleday, 1922.

Goff, May Perrin, ed. *The Household Cyclopedia*. Detroit: Detroit Free Press Publishing Co., 1886.

Green, Harvey. *The Light of the Home*. New York: Pantheon Books, 1983.

Hughes, Kristine. *The Writer's Guide to Everyday Life in Regency and Victorian England*. Cincinnati: Writer's Digest Books, 1998.

Keller, David H. *Love, Courtship, and Marriage*. New York: Roman, 1928.

Lockyer, Herbert. *Illustrated Dictionary of the Bible*. Nashville: Thomas Nelson, 1997.

MacColl, Gail, and Carol McD. Wallace. *To Marry an English Lord*. New York: Workman, 1989.

Mullins, Kathy. *Bride's Little Book of Customs and Keepsakes*. New York: Clarkson Potter, 1994.

Packer, J. I., and M. C. Tenney. *Illustrated Manners and Customs of the Bible*. Nashville: Thomas Nelson, 1980.

Panati, Charles. *Panati's Extraordinary Origins of Everyday Things*. New York: Harper & Row, 1987.

Severy, Merle. *Everyday Life in Bible Times*. National Geographic Society, 1967.

Standage, Tom. *The Victorian Internet*. New York: Berkley Books, 1998.

Stewart, Arlene Hamilton. *A Bride's Book of Wedding Traditions*. New York: Hearst Books, 1995.

Wallace, Carol McD. *All Dressed in White*. New York: Penguin Books, 2004.

Youngblood, Ed. *Nelson's New Illustrated Bible Dictionary*. New York: Nelson Reference, 1995.

index

We want to hear from you. Please send your comments about this book to us in care of zreview@zondervan.com. Thank you.

ZONDERVAN™

GRAND RAPIDS, MICHIGAN 49530 USA

ZONDERVAN.COM/
AUTHORTRACKER